FUTURE OF COMPUTERISATION IN INSTITUTIONS OF HIGHER LEARNING

BINOD C. AGRAWAL (Ph.D. The University of Wisconsin) was responsible for assessing, the effects of satellite communication in national development in India, since its inception. He taught at the Iowa State University and at the Indian Agriculture Institute. Under his leadership, "Computer Literacy and School Studies" (CLASS) project was evaluated. His publications include several books and several papers both in national and international journals. He was a member of the Indian team of the Indo-Canadian project on "Computer technology for higher education".

Currently he is President of the National Council of Development Communication.

LARRY R. SYMES (Ph.D. Purdue University) is Project Director, of the CIDA supported collaborative Indo-Canadian Project "A Design Model for Computerizing University". Dr. Symes had been Dean, Faculty of Science the University of Regina for ten years where he headed Department of Computer Science and taught since 1970. Earlier Dr. Symes taught at Purdue University. Dr. Symes is in the forefront of computerization of the institutions of higher learning in Canada. He has published extensively computer software design and evaluation of course curriculum. He has also published a number of popular articles in various computer applications.

Dr. Symes is a member of several professional associations and have travelled extensively abroad including China where he delivered invited lectures.

FUTURE OF COMPUTERISATION IN INSTITUTIONS OF HIGHER LEARNING

Edited by
BINOD C. AGRAWAL
LARRY R. SYMES

CONCEPT PUBLISHING COMPANY, NEW DELHI 110059

ISBN 81-7022-525-6

First Published 1994

Published and Printed by
Ashok Kumar Mittal
Concept Publishing Company
A/15-16, Commercial Block, Mohan Garden
NEW DELHI 110059

Lasertypeset by
Printing Express
H-13, Bali Nagar
NEW DELHI 110015

ACKNOWLEDGMENT

Several individuals and institutions contributed in organising the seminar at Surat in connection of the Indo-Canadian Computer Project between Gujarat University and the University of Regina. Our thanks are due to Dr Gunvant Shah, his team and South Gujarat University for providing all the intellectual and logistic support for holding the seminar at Surat. We take this opportunity to thank the University Grants Commission (UGC), especially Dr Madhuriben Shah, the then Chairman, UGC for providing the financial support to organize the seminar at Surat. International Development Research Centre, Canada provided financial support to enable the Canadian team to participate in the seminar. We greatly acknowledge their support. Thanks are due to Indo-Shastri Canadian Institute who assisted the Canadian team and facilitated the project activities.

All the original papers were word processed by the University of Regina, CIDA project staff. We are thankful for their invaluable help. Sincere thanks are also due to Mrs Neeta Seth who initially prepared the abstracts of the papers, provided editorial help in organizing, compiling and proof reading the manuscript. In the preparation of this book, invaluable support was provided by the staff of the Social Research Group, Space Applications Centre. We greatly appreciate their help. Last but not the least, M/s Concept Publishing Company deserve to be commended for bringing out this volume in a very short time.

BINOD C. AGRAWAL
LARRY R. SYMES

CONTENTS

SECTION III
USE AND IMPACT OF COMPUTERS

LIST OF CONTRIBUTORS

Agrawal, Binod C., Development and Educational Communication Unit, Indian Space Research Organisation, Ahmedabad, India.

Gautam, Vinayshil, Centre of Management Studies, Indian Institute of Technology, New Delhi, India.

Ghosh, Ratna, Associate Professor, Faculty of Education, McGill University, Montreal, Canada.

Gupta, Ashis, Faculty of Management, The University of Calgary, Calgary, Canada.

Jadav, Ameeta, C M C Limited, Secunderabad, India.

MacDonald, Bruce F., Associate Professor of English, Luther College, University of Regina, Regina, Saskatchewan, Canada.

Maguire, R. Brian, Computer Science Department, University of Regina, Regina, Saskatchewan, Canada.

Majumdar, B., Department of Electrical Engineering, S.V. Regional College of Engineering and Technology, Surat, India.

Miller, Roland E., Luther College, University of Regina, Regina, Saskatchewan, Canada.

Moore, Gale, Department of Sociology, University of Toronto, Toronto, Canada.

Raghavan, S.S., Reader in Computer Education, Regional College of Education, (NCERT) Mysore, India.

Reddy, P.G., Professor of Computer Science, School of Mathematics & Computer Sciences, University of Hyderabad, Hyderabad, India.

Reddy, P. Ramana, Director, Computer Centre, Sri Venkateswara University, Tirupati, India.

Reenstra-Bryant, Robin, Department of Economic Development and Trade, Regina, Saskatchewan, Canada.

Stahl, William A., Luther College, University of Regina, Regina, Saskatchewan, Canada.

Symes, L.R., Computer Science Department, University of Regina, Regina, Saskatchewan, Canada.

Thiagrajan R., Centre of Management Studies, Indian Institute of Technology, New Delhi, India.

SECTION I
GENESIS OF THE PROJECT

1

INTRODUCTION

BINOD C. AGRAWAL AND LARRY R. SYMES

This volume of edited papers has been brought out at the culmination of one of the successful collaborative research projects undertaken by Gujarat University, Ahmedabad, India and University of Regina, Regina, Canada. The papers contained herein bring together the thoughts of those who conceived and initiated the collaborative project. After the initial discussion that took place in Canade in 1985, both the Canadian and Indian scholars were of the view that a seminar in India should be organized to raise main question to be answered in the collaborative project. The paper "Genesis of the Project" by Roland E. Miller provides the historical evolution of the events that led to the seminar at Surat in 1987. Given the nature of the research venture, that too in the field of computer technology, it became imperative to define and operationalize major research issues so that they could be investigated in a broad cross-cultural perspective. The views expressed in this compilation refect the earlier thinking that went into the shaping of the actual research project between India and Canada for developing a design model for computerizing the universities.

The seminar entitled "Computer in India Universities" was organised by Dr. Gunvant Shah, Department of Education South Gujarat University at Surat from February 11-14, 1987. The aim of the seminar was to "study and assess needs, issues and strategies relevant to the introduction of computer technology; to define the key question involved; and to refine an appropriate comparative research programme that will creatively assist development in society". This is how the University of Regina team defined the objective in its initial documents prepared for the collaborative project entitled "Social Impact of High Technology on Higher Education in Saskatchewan and in an Appropriate Area in India".

Ten scholars from Canada and about a dozen from India presented papers over four days. All written papers submitted and presented are included in this volume. It would not be out of place to record the cultural shock that most Canadian team members had on arrival at Surat headed by the President of the University of Regina, Dr. Llyod Barber. This however, did not act as a determent to the enthusiasm of the Canadian team.

The semiar was divided into nine session each containing two presentations — one from Canada and the other from India (See Appendix 1). At the end of the seminar, recommendations were made based on collective discussion. All the papers have been kept in the original form in his volume with minor editorial changes except a brief presentation which has been kept in Appendix 2. Essentially this book has been divided into three sections. Section I has introduction and a single paper dealing with the aims and reasons behind holding the seminar. Section II contains seven papers related to public policy and other issues on computers and computer teaching in higher education. Section III comprises 10 papers on use and impact of computer teaching in higher education, where the authors have raised some theoretical and methodological issues in larger techno-social perspective.

Bringing out this volume, it was thought would help to keep the complete record of the collaborative project culminating at the time of the international seminar in its original form.

2

GENESIS OF THE PROJECT

ROLAND E. MILLER

It is my privilege to be able to introduce you more fully to the research project that has brought us all together here in Surat, to comment on its origin, and to outline the purpose of this seminar.

I begin by telling you a little story. I went to a neighbouring city to renew my passport. The airport was only fifteen minutes away from my location. However, I decided to telephone first to see if there was a seat available on the plane. I could not get through to the airport desk. Instead, I was switched to a city over 1,400 miles away where a distant operator looked into a monitor and informed me that there was, indeed, a seat available on the plane that was actually sitting only a few blocks from me.

But I call this experience a parable, a parable of technological good and evil. The computer did the job very well. That's good! It also cut me off from contacting a nearby human being. That's bad!

We may debate with each other the question of whether technology is totally neutral or not. I tend to the point of view that technologies which are purely destructive – let us take the production of nerve gas for example – and that have no redeeming social value, can no longer be considered purely neutral. The point is arguable. But everyone, I think, will agree that the effects of technology are not neutral. They impact on nations as a whole and on individuals within them. Those effects are both positive and negative, and the positive and negative are usually intermingled with each other. A computer can both give me my seat and cut off human communication at the same time. Here is our paradox. Here is our dilemma. The paradox is to be measured. The dilemma is to be addressed.

Most technologies that we are familiar with are well past the stage when we can address the question of their social impact with the intention of modifying the technology itself, in contrast to merely reacting to its effects. In the mega-cities in the West, we can still try to make our streets safe and liveable, but we cannot really do anything about the architectural frenzy and technology that threw up the huge sky-scrapers, creating dark canyons of despair below. That situation, it seems to me, is probably not yet true of computer technology. Here we are facing a new science that is already re-shaping and will further dramatically alter the way we do things, but which is itself at a relatively young, open and flexible stage in its development, capable of being molded, willing to be directed.

This, if true, gives us a strong reason for coming together in Surat. I am not a computer scientist, but I can recognize an impending revolution when I see one. Both our societies are facing it, in one way or the other. We must put on our thinking caps together, so that we may help each other to understand what is happening and what is still to come. We must examine to what extent we can modify the development positively, and guide it into paths and directions that are humanizing rather than de-humanizing in nature. Most certainly, we must try to grasp what all this means for education, and specifically for universities. The technology must remain the servant of human development! It is out of that kind of thinking that our project was born.

It is easy to fix a point in time for the historical genesis of this project and workshop. I will be getting to that in a moment. Let me first suggest another point which, if true, is more significant, namely, that there is a conceptual genesis for our deliberation. Any project that deals with some aspect of human technology must, in the first place, go back to and take into consideration an understanding of the relation of humanity and nature in the pursuit of truth. Here is where the great religious philosophies and thinkers of the world help us with their contributions to the understanding of this basic idea. Since I am personally involved in that field, I may be permitted a short excursion in this area.

There are two major ideas, relevant to our ensuing discussions, that merge forcefully. The first one is that the balance between the material and the spiritual must be maintained. As Professor R.N. Dandekar has put it, in reference to the Hindu view of life: "Dharma seeks to resolve the conflict between the spiritual and the material, the eternal and the temporal." (Dandekar, 1953: 131). In this light, computer technology must not be viewed simply as a mechanical technique that potentially can make life more effective and comfortable, but rather it must also be viewed in terms of its ramifications for the human spirit. The *prakrti*, the matter of the technology, as it were, must be inhabited by the *purushu,* the conscious spirit of life, and then it shall attain the balance which *dharma* seeks.

Intimately related to this idea is the warning that Jesus gave concerning the frailty of humanity, when he said: "The spirit is willing, but the flesh is weak." (St. Matthews 26: 41). It is a head-in-the-sands attitude to imagine that we can create a neutral technology that can remain neutral. It may start out neutral, but it will be operated by human beings who are less than perfect, and the technology therefore will inevitably be misused and abused. It is because he understood the weakness of humanity that Jesus prefaced the words quoted above with the stern reminder: "Keep awake!" It is a reminder that could well be written at the head of all technological advance, including that of computer technology.

An edition of *Time* magazine carried a lead article on the subject, "Why is Service so Bad?" (*Time*, 1987: 39). It chronicled the breakdown in the service industry in the U.S.A. Among other things, the article tells us about young people whose job it is to answer telephone calls from people requesting some sort of service assistance for something they have purchased. The article reports: "Computers monitor the workers' calls to measure performance. If a phone-operator spends too much time with one customer, it spoils his or her average and standing on the job. Operators have been known to fake a disconnection when customers ask questions that are too complicated." The computer is neutral, but it has become an instrument of managers who want to cut costs instead of providing reasonable service to customers, and it has become an instrument for worker oppression. The article goes on to observe "...The more that computers come into play in handling consumers, the more consumers crave reassurance that humans will intervene when help is needed."

Does the existence of these problems mean that we do not go ahead? No, because the process is irreversible. No, because our nations are committed to high tech revolutions. And above all, no, because of our belief that computer technology is already, and will be even more so in the future, a great boon for humanity. It does mean, however, that we go ahead with our eyes open. Mahatma Gandhi in his commentary on the *Gita*, wrote these prescient words:

> In regard to every action one must know the result that is expected to follow, the means thereto, and the capacity for it (M.K. Gandhi, 1972: 128).

These are really key principles for the consideration of technological activity from one who, as we all know, had deep concerns about the issue. Know the result expected, know the means available, know the human capacity. And to that Gandhiji adds the *Gita*'s primary advice – to harness knowledge with devotion.

Maintain a proper balance between matter and spirit – that is the first principle. The second principle is that the creation is for humanity, but humanity must deal responsibly with it. Everything in the universe, including that unique combination of human intellect and inert matter that equates "computer", is for humanity. In the Genesis story of the Hebrew Bible/Old Testament, God, after creating human beings, declares: "... and let them have dominion...over all the earth." (*Genesis* 1, 28). The earth, and everything in it, is meant for the benefit of humanity. Let men and women, therefore, freely and aggressively, bring forth the new technologies, and like Adam give them names, such as computer science. But the corollary is that humans must deal responsibly with the earth and its technologies. Having yielded up its gift, the earth must not be raped in return. New technology must be interdependent, and ecological and human justice must be pursued and preserved.

The *Holy Qur'an*, in one of its most poignant passages dealing with the creation, declares: "...Thy Lord said unto the angels, 'I am about to place a vice-regent on the earth'." (*Sura* 2: 29). The implication is that we are to be the stewards of the earth – its richness and its mysteries – on behalf of their true Source and on behalf of our fellow human beings on the pilgrimage of life. This passage precedes the giving of the names by Adam and, as it were, signifies the fundamental responsibility that must accompany the discovery and the promotion of technology. We must give thanks for computer technology, but then to really express gratitude we must strive to direct it so that it becomes, not an enslaving autocrat, but a true servant of human development and social justice.

This conceptual genesis of the project may not obtrude prominently in our conference, but I hope it will be there in the background to give depth to our reflections. Now let me move to the foreground. What is the precise origin of the seminar, and what are its goals and assumptions?

The project to which this seminar is related began in Regina at a meeting of the Shastri Indo-Canadian Institute, which was hosted by the University of Regina, almost three years ago. Besides members of the Institute and University, the Indian High Commissioner and a representative of the Government of Saskatchewan were in attendance. An idea grew out of the interaction that Canada and India, which have so much in common, also share some common questions and problems, ranging from soil salinity to the educated unemployed, most of which are directly related to universities. Could not a university in Saskatchewan and a counterpart institution or institutions in India collaborate on researching one of these common questions? Through such a comparative study, could we not perhaps uncover the fundamental, transcultural and universal factors underlying the selected issue and thereby make a broadly applicable contribution to societal development?

Attention soon focused on computer technology. It was the Indian High Commissioner who first underlined the critical significance of this issue and urged its possible consideration, in the light of its current importance for both nations. Things moved swiftly from there, and the project was born under the title: "The Social Impact of High Technology on Higher Education in Saskatchewan and in an Appropriate Area in India." For shorthand purposes the term "Computers in Universities" described the focus of the research project.

Support quickly gathered for the project. The Shastri Indo-Canadian Institute rendered a sponsoring and coordinating service. The University of Regina provided encouragement and gave scholarly and financial resources, the Government of Saskatchewan provided support, the International Development Research Centre granted aid for preliminary investigations as well as for Canadian participation in this Seminar; in India, the Ministry of Education and the University Grants Commission provided assistance through the formation of an Expert Committee and direct assistance towards the conduct of this Seminar, the Indian Space Research Organization graciously hosted a team from Regina, and the University of South Gujarat generously and unstintingly contributed its resources and energy by serving as the venue and host of our seminar. The breadth and depth of this support indicates, as nothing else can, the gravity of our common concern.

The project envisioned two research teams, one in India and one in Saskatchewan, independently but interactively researching the same key issues. The prominent words in the terms of reference were: comparative, reciprocal, cooperative. But what are those key issues that must be researched? It was clear that before proceeding farther, there had to be a major effort to clarify the questions that revolve around computer technology and its application in the university milieu. It was this necessity that lay behind the development of this seminar. Thus we come to the goals and assumptions that must be set out for our work.

The objectives of the seminar may be stated in the following way:

1. to study and assess needs, issues and strategies relevant to the introduction of computer technology;
2. to define the key questions involved; and
3. to refine an appropriate comparative research programme that will creatively assist development in society.

Underlying these objectives are a set of assumptions which may be expressed in the following way:

(a) That computer technology is being introduced in and will play a significant role in universities, as well as society in general;
(b) That it is necessary to evaluate the technology, to set priorities, and to optimize its appropriate application in education;
(c) That comparative study of the Indian and Canadian situations will help in the attainment of these goals;
(d) That the findings of such a comparative study may have multilateral application in the furthering of effective research, enhancement of competence and the solution of problems.

In summary then, we are not here so much in order to give each other the answers as to help each other understand the questions. That is why, after the papers have been read, at the end of the seminar, we hope to be able to have discussion in groups in which each group will discuss the following three questions:

– what are the key social and technological issues?

- what should be the university role and agenda?
- what must be further researched?

I am personally looking forward to the seminar's answer to those questions.

It is hoped that the final outcome of this seminar will be a two-year research project, involving collaborators in India and in Saskatchewan. This seminar is therefore only the opening phase of a major effort. May it be a good opening! May our minds be expanded and may also our hearts be widened one to another, as India and Canada join in an investigation that holds great potential significance for both societies, and possibly also for the wider world.

REFERENCES

Genesis 1, 28.

M.K. Gandhi, *The Gita According to Gandhi*, pp. 128-132, quoted in A.T. Embree, *The Hindu Tradition*, (New York: Vintage Books, 1972), p. 342.

R.E. Miller, unpublished design for "Surat Seminar", in "The Social Impact of High Technology on Higher Education in Saskatchewan and in an Appropriate Area in India: Computers in Universities, A Collaborative Research Project Sponsored by the Shastri Indo-Canadian Institute."

R.N. Dandekar, (1953). "The Role of Man in Hinduism," in K.W. Morgan, Ed., *The Basic Beliefs of Hinduism* (Calcutta: YMCA Publishing House, 1953), p. 131.

St. Matthew 26, 41.

Sura 2, 29.

Time, February 2, 1987, pp. 39-40.

SECTION II

COMPUTERISATION IN UNIVERSITIES
The Canadian Experience

3

PUBLIC POLICY AND HIGH TECHNOLOGY WITH SPECIAL REFERENCE TO HIGHER EDUCATION

ROBIN REENSTRA-BRYANT

During the past year and a half, I have watched this co-operative research project emerge and develop, in what is really a very short period of time. It has developed into a project that is clearly going to have the potential for generating long-term benefits for the development of the educational systems and micro-electronics industries in both Canada and India.

I would like to discuss the importance of linkages between the university, industry and government sectors, as they each try to advance learning, the general economy and the general quality of life. Each of these three sectors has its own goals, priorities and interests. But, increasingly, as world economies and increased competition limit the resources that are available to any individual group, all sectors must learn how to interact, pool their talent and resources, and how to work toward satisfying common goals.

The other papers that have been presented at this conference have focused on the goals that universities have for developing computer technologies. We have heard about research and applications that are being pursued in order:

- To improve teaching – both on and off campuses;
- To improve research; and
- To improve university administration.

Throughout all of these activities, however, the more basic goals of:

- Increasing efficiency;
- Increasing our ease of access to information; and
- Increasing the ease with which technology and knowledge can be transferred from one person to another.

are being sought.

If we look at the reasons why government and industry are pursuing the development of computer technologies, we find that governments the world over are interested in:

- The extent to which computer technologies can generate additional economic benefits to a region through both their production and applications;
- Improved efficiency for all kinds of operations (including business operations as well as educational and research processes);
- Increased opportunities for the transfer and application of new technology; and
- Improved quality of life, which in turn can attract further human resources and business activities into a region.

Industry's goals, in turn, reflect its interest in:

- The development of new technologies and products that advance the state-of-the-art, and, not incidently, increase profits and return on investments;
- Improved access to new technologies; and
- Improved prestige and enhanced corporate images, which, in turn can stimulate profits and attract more highly qualified personnel.

The difficulties of co-ordinating these different goals and objectives are alluded to in an article by Prager and Omenn in *Science* magazine. While based on observations in the U.S., their comments apply to most countries that are trying to boost their R&D outputs. They state:

"There is a growing research interest in solving critical domestic problems and a renewed appreciation for the role of industry in such problem-solving. However, the primary motivations (behind joint sector research initiatives) are more pragmatic. Academia finds itself being squeezed by its major research sponsor – the federal government. Competition for federal research funds has dramatically increased as inflation has eroded the purchasing power of the research dollar and increasing numbers of young scientists have sought support for their work. At the same time, government regulations related to scientific and financial accountability, human and animal experimentation, and biohazards have reduced the efficiency, flexibility and independence of the academic scientist. This situation is aggravated by decreasing employment opportunities in academic and government research centres and by a projected decline in student enrolments" (Prager and Omenn, 1980: 380).

As a result, co-ordination, intersectoral projects and liaison functions are frequently organized in an attempt to overcome constraints such as these.

I'd like to review some of the means by which liaisons have been forged between universities, government and industry. As John Rodman of the University of Texas has outlined in an overview of industry-university research relations, we have most frequently seen the development of:

- Improved communication techniques (including directories of faculty research interests and expertise, and of the research needs, interests and capabilities of companies);
- Industrial advisory councils;
- Visiting faculty positions for senior industrial staff;
- Consulting relationships;
- Seminars/short courses for scientists to enhance the transfer of knowledge;
- Joint research programmes;
- Facilities/equipment sharing;
- Information brokerage functions; and
- Industrial associates programmes.

In addition, governments have entered into arrangements with either academia or industry in the form of research grants, co-operative projects, and advisory committees.

What we find here is that while there are cases of bi-lateral liaisons between industry and universities, universities and government, or government and industry, tri-lateral liaisons involving all three sectors are not as frequent. Besides the difficulties of co-ordinating three separate sets of interests, priorities and agendas, tri-lateral liaisons continue to be difficult to manage during the course of the liaison.

Within Canada, a few tri-lateral programme liaisons have been developed nonetheless. In most of these tri-lateral liaisons, government often serves as a facilitator, providing funding, bringing participants together, monitoring new technology developments and encouraging technology transfer. As an example, the Canadian federal government, through its Natural Sciences and Engineering Research Council has, in recent years, sponsored university-industry co-operative research. In addition, through a new matching programme, any monies that Canadian universities receive directly from industry in support of co-operative research will generate an equivalent amount being added by the federal government to the budgets of its university granting councils. These funds, in turn, will go to further support university research efforts.

In addition to supporting a number of programmes designed to directly stimulate private sector involvement in research and technology transfer, the National Research Council of Canada is involved in tri-lateral liaisons. Through its Industrial Research Assistance Programme, it offers among its types of assistance financial support to small and medium size companies to hire university or technical students. These students are all supervised by the programme's industrial technology advisors, and they work on solutions of short-term scientific, engineering and technological problems for the companies.

Within the Province of Saskatchewan a different type of three-way liaison exists in the form of a non-profit consortium under the name of the Saskatchewan Tele-Learning Association (STELLA). This consortium has roughly 20 organizations as members, including the province's two major universities, technical institutes, provincial government departments, and co-operative organizations. The consortium uses satellites for the transmission of interactive educational programmes on a variety of topics. While satellite transmissions are generally expensive for this type of programme, the consortium approach brings costs down for particular end-users.

The Saskatchewan Government has specifically been involved in a number of initiatives to further the use of computers within the educational systems of the province. In general the addition of state-of-the-art computers to the operations of the two universities in the province has been a high priority of the government.

A Saskatchewan University Renewal and Development Fund was established in 1985 to provide $125 million for the future development of the two universities. Since the creation of the fund, priorities and plans have been set by the universities and the government for the use of some of this money. $1.65 million has been allocated to the University of Regina for the addition of computers for administrative and teaching purposes. The University of Saskatchewan has also received $7 million from this fund for a project that will generate an additional $10 million of contributions from a private sector firm. The money will be used for the development of a showcase, or model, computer system for educational purposes.

At the Province's Northern Institute of Technology in Prince Albert, Saskatchewan, a computer centre has been established by the province that will allow students to study at their own speed and enter programs at any time of the year. This module and competency-based approach utilizes an education process that is stimulated and encouraged by computers.

Within the Province's community college system, a community computer centre has been established in the City of Regina. This is a store-front operation that offers drop-in use and learning opportunities, as well as structured instruction programmes for the community.

Particular efforts to sponsor and encourage the use of computers in long-distance education have also been undertaken by the Province. At the Wascana Institute of Technology, a computer-assisted, long distance educational programme has been successfully implemented for upgrading the skills of nurses across the province. Students use computers at local colleges and through the use of telephone linkages across centralized instruction programmes.

Another programme at the University of Regina utilizes fibre optic networks to send credit and non-credit courses to students in community colleges throughout the Province. This programme involves an instructor who is viewed over a television monitor in four or five other locations and interactive voice exchanges. The system is felt to be half the cost of adding a second instructor. When the cost of the central studio is included, it is felt that the cost for adding these extra classes in remote areas will be the same as adding only one other on-campus class.

The Province's Department of Advanced Education and Manpower is currently reviewing the various issues that surround the development of distance education systems. This is being done so that:

- The province can be prepared for further developments in this area;
- Problems can be overcome in a cost-effective manner;
- Quality education can still be generated as new technological delivery systems are developed; and
- The investment already made in our existing educational infrastructure can be effectively utilized in conjunction with new technologies in the future.

In conclusion, the Province of Saskatchewan is continuing to explore a number of ways of improving the transfer, adaptation, and adoption of new knowledge and new technolgies among all sectors. Furthermore, international co-operative research projects such as this one are seen as particularly promising vehicles for such technology transfers in that they broaden the user base and increase the speed with which new knowledge and technologies are transferred.

REFERENCES

Prager, D.J., and Omenn, G.S. (1980). "Research, Innovation and University — Industry Linkage". Science, page 380.

Rodman, John A. (1983). "Industry-University Research Relations: An Overview" in Industry/University Research Relations: A Workshop for Faculty (Washington, D.C., National Science Foundation), page 4.

4

THE INFORMATION AGE AND THE MANDATE FOR RESEARCH

GALE MOORE

What's in a Name?

The Information Age is but one of a number of labels that attempt to capture the central feature of a constellation of changes that have taken place in industrially developed economies in the past 25 years. In 1959 Daniel Bell coined the term 'post-industrial society' to describe these changes (1973: 36). We have since had the Electronic Age (McLuhan, 1964), the Information Society (Kohyama, 1968), the Knowledge Society (Drucker, 1969), the Technectronic Society (Brzezinski, 1970), the Service Soceity (Gershuny and Rosengren, 1973) and the Telematic Society (Nora and Minc, 1978) to name but a few. Each name draws attention to the factor considered central to defining what is new about this period. The abundance of names suggests the diversity of opinion both on the motive force of change and on the outcomes of impacts predicted. However, in attempting to come to terms with the concept implied of consensus on the actual dimensions of change, three forces emerge as central.

First, *technological change*. This period since World War II is characterized by revolutionary changes in the technical elements of industrialised societies; the unlocking of new sources of energy from the atom and the sun, the development of new materials such as plastics and light metals, advances in transportation and communications exemplified by the exploration of space and the use of satellites, and central to all these developments, the introduction of the computer. The computer is a genuinely new technology, capable not only of extending our physical reach, but of performing tasks that replace or enhance mental activities in ways never before dreamed possible.

The word 'computer' only entered the public vocabulary in the 1950s (Roszak, 1986: 6) but with advances in transistor technology, the development of the microchip and microprocessors, this massive number crunching monster of the 1950s had become, by the 70s, a miniaturized and powerful information machine capable of storing and processing vast quantities of textural and numeric data. With the integration of this technology, both visibly and invisibly, into the public and private lives of millions around the globe, the computer became the symbol of a new age. A popular expression of this sentiment in North America was *Time* magazine's 1982 nomination of the computer as Man, or more correctly, as Machine of the Year. In making the nomination the publisher noted: "several human candidates might have represented 1982, but none symbolized the past year more richly, or will be viewed by history as more significant, than a machine: the computer" (*Time*, 1983: 3).

Second, *knowledge and information*. An assumption made by all who write about the nature of social change in industrially developed economies is that knowledge and information are key resources. The ideas that knowledge is power or that information is valuable are not new, but the conceptualization of knowledge and information as *resources* does represent a fundamental shift. As Drucker states: "There is a shift in the meaning of knowledge from an end in itself to a resource, that is, a means to some result" (Drucker, 1969: 352). Knowledge and information have become commodities, economic goods that can be exchanged in the marketplace. Bell goes so far as to say: ". . . just as capital and labor have been the central variables of industrial society, so information and knowledge are the crucial variables of post-industrial society" (Bell, 1979: 168).

Third, *structural shifts in the economic sectors*. Daniel Bell was the first to record the sectoral shift in the U.S. economy from goods-production to services. By 1960s the number of employees in the service sector surpassed the numbers employed in the goods sector, and the number of white-collar workers surpassed the number of blue-collar workers for the first time. The growth of the professional and technical occupations was outdistancing all other major occupational groups (Bell, 1973: 136). Similar shifts have been observed in the European and Japanese economies (*Information Activities. . .*, 1981: 25). An analysis of the Canadian data shows an almost identical pattern (Moore, 1986: 5-6). These structural changes have drawn attention to the place of services in advanced industrial economies and to the professional and technical workers whose tasks require the conscious application of knowledge in the performance of their duties.

In this paper, I use the name the 'Information Age', and I use it in preference to any other descriptor, for the following reasons. First, I do think that it is important to have a name around which to organize our thinking, to free us in some sense from relying on old patterns and familiar structures; to free us from industrial thinking if you like. Second, unlike many of the other names used to describe this constellation of changes, the information age does not invoke a theory of social change that predicts future outcomes. It is a generic label that captures an essential feature of what is changing and allows us to shift our focus to information and information technology, yet avoids two debates which in the short history of this field have been unproductive.

The first debate concerns the nature of social change in this period. This debate has centred on the question of whether the change is evolutionary or revolutionary. Does this constellation of changes represent a continuity or a discontinuity with the past? This is a subject with which there appears to be endless fascination, and the preoccupation with this issue obscures much of what is important. As Kumar (1978: 199) rightly asserts:

> "What needs scrutiny is the central claim that all these changes add up to a movement to a new social order, with a new set of problems, a new social framework within which to resolve them, and new social forces contending."

For example, the emphasis on technological change and sectoral shifts that have been recorded in the industrially advanced economies are often taken as sufficient evidence to support a claim of social tranformation – revolutionary change comparable to the industrial revolution. The industrial revolution was a period of major technological change, but what made it revolutionary was the constellation of social changes that occurred during that period, not the least of which was a fundamental shift in the distribution and bases of power. In feudal society, power and control resided with the nobility and landed gentry whose base of power was the control of land and labour. In industrial society, power shifted to the merchants and manufacturers whose base of control is financial capital and labour.

While theorists, such as Bell (1973, 1979), predict a change in distribution and bases of power, namely, that the professional and technical elite will gain power through control of knowledge, there is no evidence at this time to show that such processes are actually occurring. How then can we defeat the argument that this is not evolutionary change; simply a new stage of industrial development? The labelling of this period of change as revolutionary may be correct, or it may be incorrect, but in either case it is premature. In summary, it is interesting to note that the term 'industrial revolution' was coined by Arnold Toynbee in 1844, almost one hundred years after the revolution had begun in England (*Age of Access*, 1985: 32).

The second debate focuses on whether the outcome of the changes that are occurring is positive or negative. A literature review shows that there is empirical evidence to support both positions. Both the optimists and the pessimists base their predictions on partial views of the social world. The attempt to generalize obscures the important question: why are the outcomes different? Social, cultural and historical factors must be taken into account; the existing social structures analysed and the role of human agency accounted for if our studies are to be meaningful. This is sociology – the rest prophesy or ideology.

I return now to the three forces of social change to examine how these changes have been analysed in the social sciences. This analysis will inform the final section of the paper in which I will assess these changes in light of the university and the mandate for research.

Technology

There is general consensus that changes in technology, by which is meant primarily changes in material objects or tools, has been revolutionary. However, revolutionary changes in technology do not necessarily mean revolutionary, social or cultural change. These are two distinct processes of change, but neither is totally independent of the other. The first sociological studies of the impacts of computer technology in the 1960s considered technology as an independent variable. For example, the work of Blauner on alienation (1964), Woodward on organizations (1965), Mallet (1963) and other proponents of the theory of the new working class all took this approach and were criticized for technological determinism. Historical, cultural and social factors, the context of the technology, were generally not explored. Hundreds of studies followed in the 1970s – one review identified 455 items which dealt specifically with the impact of the new technology in the workplace (*Technology and the Workplace*, 1981), but by 1985, Danziger, in a review of the social science literature on the social impacts of computers, would still argue that there is a dearth of cumulative findings on this subject and that the conceptual and theoretical basis is weak. He notes: "Perhaps the main bit of theory that informs much of the recent empirical research is that the social impacts of computing are highly contingent upon *the context of use*" (Danziger, 1985: 11). While there appears to be widespread agreement that the introduction of new technology produces social changes, this generalization does not further our understanding of the process whereby such change occurs and masks the fact that while social relations are conditioned by technology, the particular application of technology will be conditioned by the existing social relations. What we must remember is that technology, as material object or tool, emerges out of a broader set of social relations and its application will be conditioned by the existing structural relations of the context – be it an organization, an institution or a nation. The relationship between technical and societal change is complex and does not only go in one direction.

Knowledge and Information

As mentioned earlier, knowledge and information have been conceptualized as resources and are expected to be the central resources of an information-based economy. There are those who see this shift as an opportunity for societies to become more egalitarian, democratic, and open. The argument is that information is unlike any other resource: it can be shared without loss to the owner, it is expandable, transportable, diffusive, i.e. difficult to monopolize, and not costly in terms of energy to produce, and therefore in abundant supply (Cleveland, 1985: 58). This position, however, overlooks the fact that while information may have these properties, the computerized storage and management of information is costly. Access to large, computerized bases or banks of information can be readily converted to a market relationship and privatization and commercialization of these databases have proceeded at a rapid pace. In addition, the enormous capacity of the computer for the manipulation of information, textual, numeric and graphic, and the amount of information which is now available in machine-readable form, has increased our reliance on this method of access, thereby increasing our dependence on the vendors of these services. This suggests the possibility of a widening gap between those with the funds to pay for this information and those who cannot. There is the potential in this situation for not only reinforcing existing patterns of inequality but for creating a new basis of inequality as the gap widens between the information rich and the information poor. The idea that knowledge and information are social goods to be used for the public good – even though some individuals have always benefited from their production and exchange – is being replaced with the idea that these are economic goods to be used for private gain.

Sectoral Shifts

The sectoral shifts observed by Bell (1973) and others in industrially developed economies are objectively measureable using census data. However, we must not fail to take into account the fact that the classification scheme used to organize and collect census and other official statistical data in most industrialised countries is industrially based. In 1940 Colin Clark published a book entitled *Conditions of Economic Progess* in which he divided economic activity into three sectors: the primary sector which includes industries based on natural resources, e.g. agriculture, fishing, forestry and mining, the secondary sector, or manufacturing industries and the tertiary sector which includes the service industries. This conceptual scheme gained acceptance not only among academics but within government agencies and this tripartite division is reflected in the industrial classification schemes developed to organize the statistical information gathered on the economies of most industrialised nations. In this scheme, the tertiary, or service sector is essentially a residual category. When the majority of the labour force is in the goods producing sector, this scheme succeeds. But as the number of industries which cannot be classified as primary or secondary continues to grow, we are left explaining the sector with the greatest variation within the framework of an industrial classification. This problem has not gone unrecognized and given the centrality of the service sector in recent theories of social change, it is not surprising that several attempts have been made to solve this problem by redefining the service sector. In one case, the service sector is subdivided into (1) a tertiary sector, which includes transportation and utilities (the blue-collar sector), (2) a quaternary sector, which includes trade, finance and real estate (the white-collar sector) and (3) a quinary sector, which includes health, education, research and government activities (the knowledge sector) (Bell, 1979: 178). In another case, a distinction is made between (1) producer services such as financial and legal services, (2) distributive services such as transportation and sales, (3) social services such as education and (4) personal services such as domestic services (Browning-Singelman Classification in Gershuny and Miles, 1983: 13-15). These schemes fail to identify the information component of the economy – a problem of some importance given the centrality of information in developed economies. In all these schemes, information activities remain scattered, not only through the service sector, but across all three sectors of the economy. An important advance in the development of a conceptual framework is the work of Mark Porat (1977) who bases his analysis of the economy on information activities which he defines as including "all the resources consumed in producing, processing and distributing information, goods and services" (Porat, 1977: 2). Porat conceives of a six-sector economy:

1. Primary Information Sector – "includes all industries which produce information machines or sell information services on (established) markets" (1977: 15).
2.&3. Secondary Information Sector – "includes most of the public bureaucracy and all the private bureaucracy" (1977: 15). The public and the private bureaucracy are each considered a sector.
4. Public Productive Sector – "that portion of Federal, State and local governments which is solely engaged in producing non-informational public and quasi-public goods" (1977: 16).
5. Private Productive Sector – "includes all market activities other than those involving information goods and services" (1977: 16).
6. Household Sector – "provides all the labor resources used by the other five sectors of the economy" ... and is "the final consumer for goods and services sold by the primary information sector and by the private productive sector" (1977: 16).

Research on the relevance of this scheme and the problems in the industrial classification to which it draws attention are important. Part of the reason it is so difficult to understand what is occurring is that we fail to conceptualize in new ways; we bring industrial models to think about questions we already suspect may not fit the model in its present form. Porat's scheme is gaining acceptance and it should be noted that this classification scheme was used in a recent OECD study which looked at information activities, electronics and telecommunications technologies in the European community (*Information Activities*. . ., 1981).

The University in the Information Age

Universities appear to be strategically placed to play an important role in the Information Age. In regard to the three major areas of change, the university is located in the industrially defined service sector, or the primary information sector if we adopt Porat's classification. Knowledge production is a central activity and information activities have been institutionalized in its libraries. In the area of technological advance and development, we note that the first computer, ENIAC, was built at the University of Pennsylvania and the first computer in Canada was built at the University of Toronto. The potential for the university to play a central role in this era was noted by Bell when he stated:

> "... just as the business firm was the key institution of the past hundred years because of its role in organizing production for the mass creation of products, the university – or some other form of a knowledge institute – will become the central institution of the next hundred years because of its role as the new source of innovation and knowledge" (Bell, 1973: 344).

There are, however, several reasons why the university may not automatically assume this role. The Information Age brings new forces to bear on this traditional institution. The high cost of staying up to date and of providing adequate resources in terms of computer and communications technology, coupled with an increasing demand for access for research, teaching and administration in virtually all departments of the univeristy, is a major pressure on university funds.

How then can the university remain at the forefront of research when the tools for research are both expensive and rapidly changing?

The state in Canada, both provincially and federally, has always been a major source of income for universities which are public institutions. In Canada, universities experienced a brief Golden Age in the 1960s as a major expansion of the university system took place. Today, however, state spending is coming under increasing scrutiny and the reduction of the national deficit has become the number one priority.

The potential for the university to play a major role in the development of the national economy has not gone unnoticed. The Science Council of Canada, a state organization, has commissioned a major study due for completion in 1987 to assess the ways in which universities can participate more effectively in economic renewal. The brochure which describes this project, in a section entitled "The University's Role in Creating Wealth", states:

> "Teaching and basic research are major roles of the university, and must remain so. But as knowledge replaces raw materials as the primer of the world's economy, the university's part in creating wealth – too often under-rated – becomes crucially important. The intellectual resources of the university are needed to help revitalize mature industries and generate the product ideas needed to create new ones. Canada's future prosperity increasingly depends on designing effective ways to integrate the university and the marketplace" (*Winning in a World Economy*, 1987).

Many universities already have links to the business community, and the negotiation of subsidies and donations with computer manufacturers is one way in which the universities have attempted to reduce the cost of providing information technology. The computer industry has seized this opportunity since the universities are a rich market – Roszak estimates that in 1984 U.S. universities spent $1.3 billion dollars on computers (1986: 57), and the university provides them with the opportunity to promote their products both to academics, many of whom are already dependent on this technology, and to students who are likely to be users of this technology in the future. Several U.S. universities, to assure that students will have access to this technology are now making ownership of a computer a condition of acceptance into the university. At Dartmouth, students must own a MacIntosh, and "Carnegie-Mellon, Drexel, Stevens Institute and Drew are among the nearly dozen schools that now add the (usually well-discounted) price of a computer into their students' tuition" (Roszak, 1986: 5). Roszak's question about this practice deserves our attention. He asks: "Has there ever been another instance of the university making the ownership of a piece of equipment mandatory for the pursuit of learning?" (1986: 58). The dependencies in this relationship between the university and the business community appear to run both ways at the present time, but I do not know of any study that has systematically investigated the implications of this relationship.

While it would be naive to believe that the university should not be accountable for the dispersion of public funds, nor is it necessarily desirable to completely isolate higher education from the structures of the economy and polity, the relative autonomy of the university is fundamentally important if the responsibility of the university to the society of which it is a part is not to be subsumed by economic or political forces. As Dahrendorf notes: "Science and technology are part of the prevailing structure of socio-economic relations in an industrial society, capitalist or otherwise, but they are at the same time a motive force for the development of a new potential for satisfying human life chances" (1977: 75). The results of research can be applied to the improvement of the life chances of the whole – a public good, or they can be turned to the advancement of private profit. The ends are a matter of choice, a question of values and the Information Age brings this issue to the fore as universities struggle with the challenge of meeting both their technological needs and their social responsibility.

The university is also an institution of teaching. The use of the computers in scientific and technical subject areas has been established for many years. With the development and diffusion of microprocessors, word processing and communications software, the use of the computers specifically, and information technologies more generally, has become widespread in the social sciences and more recently in the humanities. A humanities software fair at the University of Toronto past spring drew a large audience to the exhibits of over 35 software producers. As computer-based technologies become a part of research and study in virtually every discipline, it is essential that students are given the technical skills they need both to complete their university programs and as preparation for the job market. In Ontario, at the present time, a percentage of the students entering university are still unfamiliar with computer technology and this may be the case for several years to come. The introduction of the computer into the classroom has started at the elementary level with the result that major high schools in Toronto have poorer facilities than many of the public and secondary schools. Many of the uses of computers and information technologies, such as word processing and database creation, no longer require technical knowledge of computer programming or that students be mathematically minded. Yet, gender differences in the acceptance of this technology are still reported, with females selecting themselves out at the public school level. Computer ideology, by which I mean the set of ideas that has helped to mystify the reality of the computing environment, is slow to change. As educators, particularly in the social sciences and the humanities, the challenge is to integrate the computer and information technologies into the curriculum in such a way that they are perceived as tools; tools that are a means and not an end in themselves. The use of this technology does not abrogate the user from responsibility for thinking or responsibility for the outcome. Learning to use the computer does not constitute an education, but it can be a powerful tool in furthering that end.

We need also to think about the ethics involved in working in this new environment. Personal computers are stand alone units over which the user has a high level of control; files are private and the security of the system is quite high. However, many universities provide students access to mainframe or mini computers from which there are multiple access points through terminals connected to the system. The advantages of this configuration are that it is still less expensive than the personal computer option, the system offers high computer power, and sophisticated software is available. These systems are less secure than a personal computer; to some degree it is a public system. The problems of privacy and security are compounded once computer networks which provide communication links between users are established. There is no question that networks are incredibly useful, but as yet we do not have rules about the ethical use of these systems. For example, should individual users of a network be monitored? Should particular students be monitored if cheating is suspected? Who decides? What is the status of electronic mail? Is it personal property subject to the same rules of privacy accorded mail sent through the university mail service? Is it like the national post which can be opened if activities of a suspicious nature are expected? Who decides? Should students even have access to electronic mail systems, or only have limited access – to be able to contact their professor but not their friends? These are the theoretical questions that came out of a recent debate within one department of the University of Toronto. We must also ask what constitutes efficient and effective use of university computer resources? Should games be allowed on the system, and if so should the time at which they can be played be restricted? Should students be monitored to see that their use of the system is appropriate? What is appropriate? Again, who decides? There are no technical answers to any of these questions; the solutions are social.

In the final section of this paper I look at libraries and the changes occurring here in the Information Age. Libraries traditionally have set as their goals the collection, preservation, processing, organization and dissemination of information, a set of goals almost identical to the characteristics that define information technology. Libraries were one of the first institutions to apply computerized methods to the management of their resources. By the mid-1960s many libraries had established systems departments and library schools were introducing computer courses into the curriculum. Concurrent with these developments in library automation were developments in the computer setting of type. The large indexing and abstracting services, such as *Index Medicus* and *Psychological Abstracts*, were becoming increasingly voluminous and delays in getting these print services to the shelves of libraries were problematic. The capture of these data in machine readable form for printing coupled with the decline in cost and increased storage capacity of computers led to the early experiments with information retrieval software which could provide direct access to these files of bibliographic data. The developments in communication technology and the continuing downward trend in the cost of computer storage meant online access to these databases was not far behind. The first online databases essentially duplicated print resources. The developments taking place in libraries, for example, the MARC system which makes available cataloguing information online, met little resistance in the library community. Concerns were expressed about the integrity of the catalogue, and about the potential of job loss for cataloguers, but these problems were resolved without much conflict. The changes that were occurring supported the basic philosophy of the library community, which in North America at least, is grounded in an ideal of public service. The new technology was facilitating resource sharing and enhancing the librarians' goal of providing users with the best possible service with no cost to the user. The introduction of commercial online databases into libraries was, however, another story. There was a general consensus that libraries could not absorb the full cost of providing access to these services and that user fees would have to be charged. This issue split the library community, and is a good example of the role of values in mediating social change. For many librarians the charges incurred in accessing these databases interfered with the public right to know. The efficiency and effectiveness of the online services was never in question, but the fact that market relations were being introduced into what was held to be a public service was unacceptable to many. Information was viewed as a social good and not a material commodity. The outcome of this debate was that the commercial services did enter the library, first in the academic and special libraries and somewhat later in the public libraries and user fees became the norm. A new base of inequality had been created. As long as the online services essentially duplicated the print services, librarians could argue that the fundamental right of the public to know had not been violated, but rather that some would have access to this information more quickly than others. Today, however, an increasing quantity of information is available only online – there is no print equivalent, and there is no longer a direct correspondence between the content of all print and online files. Full-text, numeric and graphic databases are coming online and the cost of subscription to these new services is beyond the resources of most libraries. It is now estaimated that there are over 2805 public databases and databanks available online worldwide; the majority being produced in the U.S. (Williams, 1985), followed by Europe (*Encyclopedia of Information Systems and Services*, 1985). Just one American vendor, Dialog, offers over 250 databases and has 80,000 customers worldwide (*Washington Post*, May 27, 1986, A1). These estimates refer only to public data and much of the data available in this form are in private files. It is difficult to get an estimate of the number and size of these proprietary files. Schiller estimates that in 1979 two-thirds of all records held in organized databases were located in U.S. bases, and of this the government owned approximately 25 per cent, the remainder being held privately (Schiller, 1981: 36). The content of these databases reflects the interests of the producers. The implications of this have not gone unrecognized. Nora and Minc in their 1978 report to the French government raise this concern.

They state:

> "Information is inseparable from its organization and its mode of storage. In the long run, it is not only a question of the advantage that may be conferred by familiarity with such and such a set of data. Knowledge will end up being shaped, as it always has been, by the available stock of information. Leaving to others – i.e. to American banks – the responsibility for organizing this 'collective memory' while being content to plumb it is to accept a form of cultural alienation. Installing data banks is an imperative of national sovereignty" (1980: 80).

With the world community linked into a global communications network, and the establishment of foreign centres licensed to provide access to American and European databases, the path of least resistance is a difficult and costly one not to follow. Statistics on the use of these online services are not readily available since this information belongs to the vendors who are not obligated to disclose it. Aggregate data for the major online vendors of word-oriented databases in the U.S. information centre/library market have been compiled and give some idea of the usage and revenue generated by these systems. In the fourth quarter of 1982, 315,000 hours generating 33.5 million dollars were logged. By the first quarter of 1985, these figures had jumped to 567,000 hours with revenues of 63.8 million dollars (IT to Publish..., 1986: 30). I include one example of the use of a single vendor. In October 1986, the National Library of Medicine in Bethesda, Maryland celebrated the fifteenth anniversary of MEDLINE, a medicial database, with one free day of searching for users of this file. Sixteen hundred and thirty hours were logged by American and foreign centres during the twenty-four hour period (Records Broken..., 1986: 11).

The cost of accessing these databases consists of three major charges – a fee for the producer of the database, a fee for the vendor who provides the information retrieval software and the accounting system and a fee for use of a communication utility. In the United States the majority of distributors and a large number of the producers are private firms. There are government producers; MEDLARS, the medical information system and ERIC, an education service are two examples and MEDLARS is distributed by the National Library of Medicine, a state institution. The cost of accessing government produced and/or vended information is lower than for the commercial services as the state has taken the position that data collected and made available through public funding should not be subject to market relations in its pricing. By the beginning of the 1980s a major debate on the issue of public sector/private sector provision of information services was underway as commercial vendors charged that the lower priced government database services represented unfair competition. The National Commission on Libraries and Information Science reported on this issue in 1982, but there was no clear resolution. This is an important issue for universities as well, since innovations produced in the university are often commercially viable. There are, in Canada, examples of university funded projects that have been privatized. UTLAS International Inc., a worldwide vendor of library cataloguing has been a private corporation since it separated from the University of Toronto in 1985. Part of the resources of this firm, which they vend for a fee, are the machine-readable files of the university library and system software which were produced during the time this organization was part of the university. QL Systems is a private firm which today vends over 100 databases. The original development of this system was undertaken at Queen's University in Kingston, Ontario. This is not to suggest that privatization is not in the best interests of the university, but rather to suggest that the implications of the conceptualization of knowledge and information as resources require new responses from the university to assure that information and knowledge produced at public expense is recovered by the public through lower charges or through funds returned to public institutions.

The growing privatization and commercialization of information has not gone unnoticed in the United States. There is growing concern that increased government use of private sector contractors and consultants for data gathering and analysis means that information collected at public expense is not entering the public domain. Libararies which act as depositories for U.S. government material increasingly find that the reports and documents they require must be purchased from private research organizations, and often at very high cost (Schiller, 1981: 58). The role of the library as a public watchdog on these activities is important, but it is unlikely that libarians can stem the tide without a broader base of support. The private troubles of librarians must become public issues in the 80s if the public right to know is not to be lost.

Since the early 1980s end-user searching of online databases has emerged as an important issue. End-user searching is online searching done by the person who requires the information – a trained search intermediary is not used. The diffusion of personal computers, increased friendliness and ease of use of the software packages and the development of gateways – a single entry point to a variety of vendors – has reduced the complexity of online searching. As more and more users become familiar with the online environment, perhaps there will be increased concern with some of the issues noted above. However, as the most extensive use will probably be in North America and Europe, concerns about content, cost and the politics of information technology may be slow to emerge. In April 1986, the University of Toronto Library Subcommittee on End-User Searching was formed. It is interesting to note that the terms of reference focused exclusively on the administrative and technical aspects of activity – the problem of content and issue of inequality that had been so central a few years before had disappeared.

The politics of information technology will be a major issue of the second half of the 1980s and beyond. To go beyond the university for a moment, we can see that the user of information technologies has extended far beyond the collection and dissemination of public databases. The use of remote sensing devices and satellites makes it now possible to invisibly gather data from around the world, and the world communication system makes possible its dissemination. The key questions of the future will focus on control – technology provides the means but it cannot tell us what we ought to do. There is a power capacity inherent in this technology to improve the lives of millions around the globe, but there is also the possibility of a new form of imperialism – a form made all the more powerful by the fact that its infrastructure is largely invisible.

In conclusion, I return to the original question of the role of the university in the Information Age and the mandate for research. I conclude with the following thought. The university as a centre of knowledge production and information activities has the technical expertise to play a major role in the Information Age, but the big questions about the future are not technical questions but questions of human will – the challenge is to work towards ends that utilize these means in a socially responsible way.

REFERENCES

Age of Access: Information Technology and Social Revolution. Posthumous Papers of Colin Cherry. W. Edmondson. London: Croom Helm.

Bell, D. (1973). *The Coming of Post-Industrial Society: A Venture in Social Forecasting*. New York: Basic Books.

Bell, D. (1979). "The Social Framework of the Information Society." In *the Computer Age: A Twenty-Year View*, edited by M. Dertouzos and J. Moses, Cambridge, Mass., MIT Press, 163-211.

Blauner, R. (1964). *Alienation and Freedom: The Factory Worker and His Industry*. Chicago: University of Chicago Press.

Brazezinski, Z. (1970). *Between Two Ages: America's Role in the Technetronic Era*. New York: Viking.

Clark, C. (1940). *The Conditions of Economic Progress*. London: Macmillan.

Cleveland, H. (1985). "The Twilight of Hierarchy: Speculations on the Global Information Society." In *Information Technologies and Social Transformation*, Washington, D.C.: NAS Press.

Dahrendort, R. (1977). "Observations on Science and Technology in a Changing Socio-Economic Climate." In *Scientific-Technological Revolution: Social Aspects*, London: Sage, 73-82. (Sage Studies in International Sociology, 8).

Danziger, J. (1985). "Social Science and the Social Impacts of Computer Technology." *Social Science Quarterly*, 66: 3-21.

Drucker, P. (1969). *The Age of Discontinuity: Guidelines to Our Changing Society*. New York: Harper & Row.

Encyclopedia of Information Systems and Services (1985). 1985-86 ed. Detroit: Gale Research. 2 vols.

Gershuny, J. and Miles, I. (1983). *The New Service Economy: The Transformation of Employment in Industrial Societies*. London: F. Pinter.

Gershuny, J. and Rosengren, W.R. (1973). *The Service Society*. Morrlstown, N.J.: Schenkman Pub. Co.

Information Activities, Electronica and Telecommunication Technologies. (1981). Vol. 1. Paris: OECD. (Information Computer Communication Policy, 6).

"IT to Publish Quarterly Database Usage Figures". *Information Today*, Nov. 1986.

Kohyama, K. (1968). "Introduction to Information Society Theory." *Chuo Koron*. Cited by Y. Masuda in *Changing Value Patterns and Their Impact on Economic Structure* cited in M. Marien, 1984, "Some Questions for the Information Society," *The Information Society*, 3:183.

Kumar, K. (1978). *Prophecy and Progress: The Sociology of Industrial and Post-Industrial Society*. London: Allen Lane.

Mallet, S. (1975). *The New Working Class*. Nottingham: Spokesman Books.

McLuhan, M. (1964). *Understanding Media: The Extensions of Man*. New York: McGraw-Hill.

Moore, G. (1986). Post-Industrialism: An Analytical Model Towards the Study of Social Control. Unpublished manuscript.

National Commission on Libraries and Information Science. (1982). *Public Sector/Private Sector Interaction in Providing Information sergvices*. Washington, D.C.: Supt. Docs.

Nora, S. and Minc, A. (1980). *The Computerization of Society: A Report to the President of France*. Cambridge, Mass.: MIT Press.

Porat, M. (1977). *The Information Economy: Definition and Measurement*. Washington, D.C.: Dept. of Commerce, Office of Telecommunications.

"Records Broken on MEDLINE Anniversary." (1986). *National Library of Medicine News*, 41: no. 12.

Roszak, T. (1986). *The Cult of Information: The Folklore of Computers and the True Art of Thinking*. New York: Pantheon Books.

Schiller, H. (1981). *Who Knows: Information in the Age of the Fortune 500*. Norwood, N.J.: ABLEX Pub. Corp.

Technology and the Workplace (1981). Sydney: New South Wales Ministry of Technology.

Times: The Weekly Newsmagazine, *121: no. 1, Jan. 3, 1983.*

5

COMPUTER TECHNOLOGY IN HIGHER EDUCATION IN CANADA

L.R. SYMES

Introduction

Computing equipment was first introduced to a few Canadian university campuses in the 1950s. By the 1960s some form of computing was generally installed on all university campuses. Today, while computing is available on all campuses, it is not universally employed. The three main reasons for this are:

1) the lack of certain types of services,
2) the lack of capacity, and
3) the Luddite attitude of certain members of the faculty.

Before investigating how and where computing fits into a Canadian university, one must ask why (Final Report, 1986, Interim Report, 1985). The mission statement for the University of Regina is typical of mission statements for a Canadian university. It says in part:

> "The purpose of the University is the preservation, transmission, interpretation and enhancement of the cultural, scientific and artistic heritage of the human race, and the acquisition and expansion of new knowledge and understanding.
>
> The University of Regina believes that it can best provide this quality of education by designing programmes that build on solid foundations of intellectual experience. Students will be prepared for the requirements of society and the demands of a world in which the rapid advancements in knowledge will have to be un-

derstood and applied in ways which are consistent with the higher human values."

In order to meet this responsibility, a university must provide students with ready access to computing and communication tools and services which will enhance their studies and learning experience. This requirement is further necessitated when account is taken both of the impact which technology is having on society, and of the growing expectation that university graduates will be familiar with modern technology.

Access to suitable computing and communication tools and services is also essential in achieving the research objectives of almost all disciplines. While this need may vary from the requirement to compute, to the necessity to store and access information, its importance is becoming ever more obvious to individual faculty members who wish to remain at the forefront of their discipline.

Finally, if a university is to meet its educational and research objectives it must discharge its managerial responsibilities efficiently and economically. To do this in the 1980s requires an ever-increasing reliance on computing and communication tools to support administrative functions such as student services, payroll and accounting.

Administrative Structures

When the first computer arrived on a campus, it was usually managed by the individual that made the case for its acquisition. This was typically a professor in either the mathematics or physics department of the institution.

As additional academic and administrative users attempted to gain access, this management structure was modified by the creation of some form of a computing advisory committee. This in turn led to the creation of a separate unit on campus called the Computer Centre, which was responsible for providing for both the academic and administrative computing needs of the university.

On many campuses this structure, the single computer centre, broke down, and two separate computer centres were created – one to provide for academic computing, and the other to provide for administrative computing. Typically, these units had their own computing equipment as well as their own staff.

The primary cause for the creation of two computer centres on a campus was the dramatic growth of administrative computing. As the administrative load grew, the perception on the part of academic users was that their needs were not being satisfied, because of the demands and the control exerted by administrative users.

Today with the diversity of users and the options that exist for satisfying their needs, users can no longer be divided simply into administrative and academic computing. A new category of computing has appeared (re-appeared) on campus, owing to the introduction of the minicomputer and later the microcomputer – the locally controlled and operated system.

Therefore, today there are four distinct components that must be accounted for and managed in a campus computing resources pool. These are:

(1) Academic – Centrally Supplied
(2) Academic – Locally Supplied
(3) Administrative – Centrally Supplied
(4) Administrative – Locally Supplied

Ignoring for our purposes the day-to-day management of each of these units, we can see that a mechanism is required to control growth. This control can vary from having each and every purchase approved by an individual or central group, to having approval implicitly given when budgets are allocated. This problem of managing relative growth, combined with the rising importance of computing to the academic and administrative health of a univeristy, has prompted some institutions to merge their two computer centres back into one – or at least to designate a senior administrative officer as being responsible for computing on campus.

The term 'academic computing' is used to describe two distinct activities – instructional computing and research computing. While campus computing has been formally subdivided into administrative and academic computing, academic computing has not been separated into instructional and research computing. The result of this situation is that the instructional computing needs of an institution have frequently dictated what is available for research. The computational research needs of the campus are satisfied by providing the researchers with access to the machine that was acquired, primarily, to support the instructional requirements. Further, research users are usually 'allowed to access' only the computer time that is not consumed by instructional computing. If campus computing has not been separated into academic and administrative units, the problems are even more severe for the researcher who is attempting to use computing, because he must compete with both instructional and administrative computing to acquire the resources required.

The minicomputer, and later the microcomputer, provided the researchers with their first real opportunity to select what they wanted. Many have taken advantage of this opportunity, but not always with the anticipated result. One of the undesirable by-products of this course of action is that the researcher, instead of enhancing productivity, actually inhibits it, because attention has been diverted from the actual research project to learning how to use the machine. In some cases, productivity has been further diminished if the need for computing outgrew the capacity of the machine, because if the researcher continues to use the small machine past the point of its capacity, he is forced into the position of having to make the problem fit the machine. This in turn requires him to learn even more about the machine, at the expense of actual research time.

Finances

Today it is not uncommon for the computing budget of a university to account for four per cent of the institution's operating budget. This can be translated as an expenditure on computing of $600.00 per undergraduate student (Interim Report, 1985).

Omitting how administrative computing is budgeted or accounted for, the method employed to control, encourage and pay for academic computing can be classified as being one of the following three schemes:

(1) no accounting,
(2) centralized budgeting, and
(3) decentralized budgeting.

Under the no accounting scheme, users are provided with a computing account number and are assigned with resources limited in some way to control their utilization, such as: the amount of disk space they can use, the size of job they can run, and the type of services they can access. From there on, computing is seen from the user perspective as being a free resource, to be consumed as required to the available capacity.

The centralized budgeting model attempts to provide for better control of usage by allocating funds to individual users or departments from the computer centre's budget. These funds can then only be used to purchase units of computing from the computer centre.

With a decentralized budget, individual users or department units have funds in their own budgets with which they can purchase computing. These funds can then be used to purchase service from the computer centre or from other service bureaus, or to create local facilities. Depending upon the level of decentralization and control, these funds may be used to purchase non-computing resources.

It should be noted that when budgeting is performed, the charging policy adopted usually employs a variable rate structure so as to encourage the distribution of demand across the day. Typically, the rate charged is highest during normal working hours and lowest after mid-night.

The financial pressures of the 1980s gave rise to the discovery of a new financial base – the student. One scheme involves allocating to students certain funds for the purchase of computing resources. If they require more, they must purchase the 'extra' resource themselves, usually at a heavily discounted rate. Another scheme involves the assessment of computing fees for all students. A third plan involves encouraging the students to purchase their own equipment.

The problem of the funding of computing is further complicated by two factors. First, funding of education in Canada is a provincial responsibility. However, a great deal of the funding for research, done at universities, comes from the granting bodies which are, in turn, funded by the federal government. Consequently, changes in policies at the federal level can have a significant effect. This was vividly witnessed in the early 1970s when the major granting body, which provides support to researchers in the sciences and engineering, changed its policy for supporting research computing. Their policy was changed from one which provided universities with a block grant to cover the cost of research computing to one which allocated funds directly to researchers which they, in turn, could use to purchase the computing they required. This change forced institutions where there was no charging policy to adopt one, and frequently resulted in less revenue being available to the computer centre because researchers set up local facilities or claimed, with some justification, that their grants did not contain sufficient monies to purchase the computing they required.

Second, universities receive the majority of their funding from their provincial governments in two forms – operating grants and capital grants. Computing growth and stability can be dramatically affected by the type of grant which is paying for computing. If equipment is obtained from funds provided in capital grant, institutions frequently find themselves on a roller coaster which goes from feast to famine. When they get a grant for new equipment they feast, but all too often the next capital grant for equipment comes only after a period of famine.

An associated problem is the funding of local facilities on campus. At the University of Regina, capital funds have been allocated to faculties or departments to permit them to establish a local computing facility. When institutions do this, care must be taken to insure that these units have determined for themselves the ways in which they are going to reallocate existing operating funds to provide for maintenance and operation of the local facility. Alternatively, additional funding must be provided to these units.

Technology

How has technology affected the delivery of services to students and staff? Before looking at specific effects, the two examples below give an indication of the rate of change:

Example (i) Computing Power

The following table (Datamation, 1984: 159) gives the raw computing power, measured in millions of instructions per second (MIPS), that can be derived from a number of IBM mainframes which were delivered during a 25-year period.

DATE	MACHINE	MIPS
Sept/58	7070	0.022
April/65	360/65	0.680
Aug/72	370/168	2.3
Feb/77	3033	4.7
Sept/82	3084	26.0

The actual power of an individual machine is not as significant as the rate of change. The above table shows that there was a 1000 fold, three orders of magnitude, increase in processor speed in the 25-year period from 1958 through 1982.

Example (ii) Cost

In 1970, the University of Regina had as its central computer an IBM 360/40 with 128 k bytes of main memory. This machine was leased for approximately $17,000 per month. In 1983, IBM introduced a microcomputer called the PC/XT/370. This machine was capable of running the same programs as the mainframe the University had 13 years earlier, twice as fast, with six times the amount of memory, and its purchase price was only 2/3 the monthly lease of the 360/40.

The pace of change has made the impossible possible – from both the perspectives of cost and of capacity.

With the change from batch to online interactive machines, keypunches were replaced with terminals, and the need for communication facilities was introduced. When online machines were initially introduced, their associated terminals were physically attached or, in exceptional cases, were permitted to use the telephone system to make the connection. As the number of online systems grew, the requirement to install some form of terminal switching capability became more and more apparent. Each machine which was acquired had a certain portion of the campus load and service requirement assigned to it. This led to the situation where a user was required to gain access to different machines for different tasks. Terminal switching was therefore required to avoid the problem of having the user move from terminal to terminal to access the different machines, or the problem of having terminals idle on one machine while there are more users than terminals wanting to get on another machine. The telephone system could not handle this type of service because it was never designed to handle a large number of simultaneous calls that last for a long period of time. The result was the appearance on campus of a new service – the terminal/data switch with its own set of communications lines.

The need for communications has continued to grow with the expansion of local computing facilities. Local area networks are now being developed to provide users with the ability to move files (work) from one machine to another and to access other machines on the network without using the teminal switch (Stevenson, 1985, Kaliniuk, 1986).

The microcomputer introduced a number of unique problems, perhaps the most important of which is deciding what machines users should be encouraged to acquire? In the absence of any acquisition policy, users will ultimately acquire one of almost every type of machine. If this should occur, how are users going to obtain maintenance support for their machine, and can the campus provide them with the software consulting service they require? The answer is, of course, 'no'.

The adoption of an acquisition policy should not be viewed as being restrictive, but should be seen rather as a guide to tell the users what types of machines and software products the institution is capable of supporting. If a user needs to purchase a system which is not on the 'approved' list, this can be done, but the user cannot expect to be given the same level of support that is provided to a user that has acquired a system from the approved list.

Trends

With the introduction of the minicomputer and later the microcomputer, Canadian universities saw the re-creation of computing units dedicated to a single academic discipline. Computer Science Departments were among the first disciplines to take this course, as they needed to be able to provide their students with direct access to the operating system, something which could not be accommodated on a shared central facility.

As prices have come down, similar dedicated facilities have been introduced by other academic units. These have all been justified by either the uniqueness of the provided service, or by the level of local utilization. Proposals to establish such facilities must, however, be reviewed carefully. Once such a facility has been created, it is not likely that it will be shared to the same extent as centrally provided service.

Of particular concern is the establishment of microcomputer laboratories. It is normal for academic units as well as individual faculty members to want their own. However, it may be better to adopt a policy whereby the computer centre provides for their needs. If this is done, accessibility by a number of different user groups is ensured, costs are reduced, and the level and array of service may be enhanced.

There is a growing number of universities in North America where engineering students in particular are being encouraged to purchase their own microcomputers. Even at institutions where there is no such policy, the number of students who are acquiring their own microcomputers is increasing. This activity forces the institution to pay more attention to their communications facilities. Once students have their own machines, they need to be able to access the university's systems from a number of different locations, including their own residences.

The microcomputer has also affected office automation. Early word processing systems used a central computer and a terminal. However, a microcomputer can provide all the service locally. If microcomputers are used, what, if any, guidelines should be adopted? This question is complicated by the fact that the type of word processing system required by the Departments of Chemistry and Mathematics is normally different from the word processing system required by the Department of English and the Vice-Chancellor's Office. In the absence of a standard being adopted by the institution, each unit or group of units will choose a system which meets their own needs. This process leads to incompatibility. Staff must be retrained should they move from one office to another. Work cannot easily be shared between office groups. And answers must, ultimately, be found for questions regarding such matters as maintenance for a wide array of unique systems and access from this array of systems to special pieces of equipment (such as a laser printer).

At the other end of the spectrum, Canada has two supercomputers (*Waterloo Newsletter*, 1986) installed in universities – University of Calgary and University of Toronto. They have been justified and funded by provincial governments on the basis of providing service to their own research users and service to industry in the neighbourhood of the university, which requires this type of computing.

This model is quite different from what has been adopted in the United States. There they created an academic computer network in the 1970s and have expanded its capacity during the past few years by the installation of a number of supercomputers in universities which are nodes on the network.

The question of networks and supercomputer access is of great importance, for individual researchers will always require computing capacity that cannot easily be satisfied by their local computer centre.

A Canadian computer network, NETNORTH, was created in 1984 with the support of IBM. This network does not currently provide researchers with the option to access and use remote computing capacity, but it does allow faculty members, in Canada, to communicate with one another electronically and to do this with others around the world through gateways to other national computer networks. While this type of network greatly enhances collaborative research activity, it does not solve the above-mentioned problem of running large jobs.

Electronic mail is also starting to be used by a number of different user groups for communications on campus. Administrators and faculty members are using it to communicate with one another instead of using the telephone, and students are using it outside of the normal office hours to ask questions of faculty members.

Conclusions

Given today's rapidly changing environment, a university's approach to managing its computing facilities must be equally flexible and responsive to change. Temporarily at least, the expansion of microcomputer usage has expanded demand for centralized facilities. Thus, there has been minimal conflict between the growth in the use of microcomputers by individual faculty members and the continued growth of the computer centre. However, as technology continues to change, university administrators must find the time, energy, and expertise to manage technology – as opposed to being driven by it.

REFERENCES

Dagani, R. (1985). Supercomputers Helping Scientists Crack Massive Problems Faster, *Chemical and Engineering News*.

Dougherty, D.M. (1983). Academic Computing: The State of the Art in Equipment, Organization, and the Trend to Terminal Use and Networking, *Association for Educational Data Systems Journal*.

Final Report of the President's Advisory Committee on Information Technology and Services, The University of Western Ontario, March 1986.

Interim Report of the President's Advisory Committee on Information Technology and Services, The University of Western Ontario, 1985.

Kalyniuk, Todd H. (1986). Design and Analysis of an Integrated Communications Network, M.Sc. Thesis, University of Regina.

McCredic, John W. (1983). *Campus Computing Strategies,*, Editor, Digital Press.

Stevenson, G.H. (1985). The Design and Implementation of a Local Area Network in a Multiple Operating System Environment, 1984, M.Sc. Thesis, University of Regina.

The Cray Supercomputer at the University of Toronto, Dept. of Computing Services, *University of Waterloo Newsletter #52*, March 1986.

Wiener, Hesh (1984). Mainframe Manoeuvers, *Datamation,* pp. 159-166.

6

THE POTENTIAL OF A COMPUTER AS A TOOL IN HIGHER EDUCATION

AMEETA JADAV

In recent years, there has been a tremendous growth in the use of computers in education. This has perhaps been facilitated by the introduction of micro and mini computers in the market and the relative ease of obtaining them. With this increase in interest, software publishers have been flooding the market with educational software on a variety of subjects and of varying quality. These software deal with different educational applications. Many software programmes 'teach' the learner, others are programming languages through which a user communicates with the computer and some are aids which help the user in carrying out certain tasks such as accounting and record keeping. A widely accepted classification of educational application of computers was given by Taylor (1980). He suggested that the computers could be used as tutor, tutee and tool in education.

In this paper, I would like to discuss the potential of the computer as a tool in higher education. However, before doing that, let me briefly discuss what each of the applications identified by Taylor, i.e. tutor, tutee and tool, refer to.

The use of a computer as a *tutor* refers to the application wherein the computer acts as the teacher and 'teaches' the learner through tutorials, simulations, games, drill and practice or a combination of any of these strategies. The potential of computers in this role is very high and has already been researched and written about a great deal. It is in reference to this role that many popular terms such as Computer Assisted Instruction – CAI, Computer Based Training – CBT, Computer Based Education – CBE, and so on, have been used. A major strength of the computer in this role is individualization of instruction.

In the *tutee* application, the learner teaches the computer how to carry out certain procedures by using a programming language. In this process, the learner studies a procedure and breaks it down to the simplest of steps which can be communicated to the computer. In doing so, concepts are clarified, insights are developed and an understanding of the procedures is gained. This aspect has been explored in detail, with respect to young children, by Seymour Papert and his associates through the development and use of a programming language known as LOGO (Papert, 1980).

And now I come to the third application, which is the focus of this paper – the use of the computer as *a tool*.

Tools such as shovels, plows, bicycles, automobiles, washing machines, pencils, typewriters, pianos, and so on, which mankind has designed and developed in the past, have helped us to extend our physical capabilities. In the role of a tool, the computer gives us the ability of extending our mental capabilities. In this sense, it is different from the other tools, but basically its purpose is to make life simpler, easier and generally give us the freedom to use our time in activities of our choice.

If we consider higher education, the main focus of activities is on learning through research and instructional presentations (both classroom and through seminars and meetings such as this one). Furthermore, administration units in colleges and universities help by providing support services and maintaining co-ordination between the various activities of the institution. In our universities, the computer can be used as a tool in all these three functions, i.e. research, instruction and administration. In western countries, the computer has been used by universities in all these functions and it has been accepted as an important and virtually indispensable tool for smooth functioning of these institutions.

At this point, I would like to stress that as a tool, the computer is not likely to take away jobs (as is popularly believed), but rather to take care of mundane, iterative, time-consuming tasks and carry them out accurately, at a great speed and if necessary, repeat them for an unlimited number of times. Of course, it is likely that their introduction in institutions would require training of personnel in computer related skills. At the same time, there might also be a need to contend with some attitudinal blocks which are invariably faced by any innovation which leads to a change.

It is generally agreed that a vast amount of time in our universities goes toward repetitive, procedural tasks and the efficiency rate of our personnel in these tasks is not something we would like to boast about. Under such circumstances, it might be beneficial to examine an alternative such as computerisation which has the potential of adding efficiency and speed and at the same time is likely to make the tasks easier to perform.

Let us look at some of the tasks that a computer can perform for the functions of research, instruction and administration in Indian Universities.

Research

If we consider the process of conducting research, we come across many time-consuming tasks such as literature searches, record keeping during the conduct of research, data analysis and report writing. The computer has been found to contribute greatly in simplifying and speeding up these tasks. It has also been found very useful in conducting pilot tests by simulating situations under study and also in controlling the conduct of actual experiments. Let us examine these in detail.

Literature Searches

Computerised catalogues in the university libraries can be used for quick location of reference materials (books and journals) for specified subjects and topics. Under such systems, we could enter a topic name in a computer and get a list of books and journals in the library on that topic. At the same time, if we are looking for a specific book or author, it should be just as easy to locate the call number by using the computer.

Secondly, abstracts of articles from journals and other publications can be located by specifying critical descripters (example – ERIC). This type of literature search service can be provided on a regular basis to researchers (monthly bulletins) or can be invoked for specific requests.

Simulation of Process under Study for Pilot Tests

Certain research studies – especially in the field of advanced physics, chemistry, biology and mathematics, can become extremely expensive because of the cost of the materials and equipment required to conduct them. It is often possible in such cases to simulate the process under study through carefully written software and try out the effects of different combinations of variables. The outcomes of these simulated processes can be recorded and decisions about conducting the actual experiment/study could be taken. The researcher can conduct these pilot tests relatively cheaply and also avoid other hardships that might occur in conducting the actual tests.

Control of Research Processes

When a research process requires changes in the value of independent variables on a regular basis (such as temperature, pressure, rate of flow), the computer can automatically control the process and make the necessary changes as and when specified in the programme. While doing this, it can also keep recording the values of the dependent variables – as is discussed next.

Record-keeping During the Conduct of Research

An organised record-keeping can be carried out using the computer programmes which have been created specifically for these purposes. These records can be maintained in such a way as to make data analysis simple and convenient. The process of record-keeping can be automatic (i.e. the computer automatically records the values) or manual, in which the values are entered by the researchers.

Data Analysis

A number of researchers in our universities have most probably experienced a few nightmares when carrying out data analysis for their research projects. Many specialised statistical data analysis packages are available on the computer which allow speedy and error-free data analysis. An additional advantage of using computerized data analysis is that one can carry out a number of exploratory analyses for the data and thereby add richness to the findings of the study.

Report Writing

This final stage of a research project can often end up being a herculean task – especially when a series of drafts have to be prepared before the final version of the report is produced. Typewritten reports have to be typed all over again each time a new draft is produced. Secondly, it is very difficult to neatly correct a typing error on paper. Computerised word-processing helps in avoiding these problems. The document is saved on a disc and modifications can be made in any part of the document with minimal effort. Because of this facility, corrections are also made on the computer and this leads to production of a neat and organised report.

When the report includes tables, charts, graphs and diagrams, the process of producing and modifying can also become quite a time-consuming and tedious task. Graphics programmes on the computer can help produce graphics and make minor as well as major modifications in them with relative ease.

This simplification of the process of writing could also help in improving the quality of the material (that is, the content of the report) that is produced. I am firmly convinced that this particular application can prove to be one of the greatest boons to researchers.

Now let us examine some ways in which a computer can help in the instructional presentations, both in classroom situations and also for seminars and symposiums.

Instruction

The instructors in our universities spend a number of hours in locating reference materials, preparing presentations, preparing instructional aids, developing tests, analysing the test responses, maintaining and updating records, and so on. Let us see how a computer can help in these tasks.

Locating Reference Materials

As was mentioned earlier, the introduction of computerisation in the university libraries can simplify the process of locating reference materials. This service can prove to be highly advantageous to instructors.

Organisation of Notes

Computerised filing systems can help in organisation of notes on various topics. These notes can be classified in accordance with topics and can be easily modified from time to time. This is likely to help us in easily maintaining up to date notes on various topics. All good filing programmes also provide the facility of printing out these notes when required.

Preparation of Instructional Aids

Word-processors can be used to prepare and modify student handouts. Graphics programmes can be used to prepare diagrams and figures for these handouts. Paper copies for the production of overhead transparencies can also be efficiently prepared using the graphics programmes.

Computerised Testing

Most instructors would agree that the process of testing is a crucial one in instruction. However, this is also one of the most time-consuming processes. Besides, as we all know, development of a reliable and valid testing instrument requires careful preparation, revisions and test result analyses. If computers are enlisted as aides in this process, they can help in the following ways:

1. Creation of an item bank wherein each item is placed in a grid on the basis of type of question, sub-topic, difficulty level and so on. This information can be saved on a tape or a disc and modified from time to time as required.
2. Development of a test. In accordance with the specifications given to the computer, tests can be developed from the item bank. The instructor may decide to randomly select the items from the item bank or choose each item individually.
3. Conduct of a test. We can foresee a time when students will respond to objective questions on the computer or on a computer sheet. Their responses can be immediately matched with the correct response and a test result can be produced for each student in a matter of seconds. This will save the instructor the time and effort spent in manual checking of the test responses and the associated calculations and result preparations.
4. Item Analysis. These routines can be utilised to get information such as the difficulty value and discrimination index of the items. Modification of items can be based on this analysis.

In addition to the above applications, instructors are likely to find the computer a very helpful tool for record keeping of student scores, attendance, assignments and so on (Merrill, Tolman, Christensen, Hammons, Vincent and Reynolds, 1986).

Administration

University and college administrations involve a lot of record-keeping, financial planning, scheduling exercises and so on. In these tasks, a computer has been found to be useful to a large extent. While it would be difficult to review all the possible ways in which a computer could be used in administration, I would like to mention a few in which the contribution of computers is most widely felt.

Record-keeping

One of the chief responsibilities of university administration units is to maintain records for students, staff and university activities. We have all probably experienced claustrophobia on entering one of the records offices in administration buildings of our universities. The files containing records are piled thick and high in these offices, and locating a file and extracting specific information becomes a superhuman task. With the introduction of computerisation, one is likely to see vast savings in terms of space and paper and, of course, time and effort of the records office staff. No longer will it be necessary to maintain thick files of information. Magnetic media will store the information and whenever required, a paper copy of the record will be printed. No doubt, the process of record keeping itself will become simpler with computer programmes for data based management and filing. Getting a transcript or marks sheet has been found to become a matter of minutes under computerised record-keeping. Computerisation could also help in the reduction of red tape that is generally associated with these tasks. However, this aspect would be more an outcome of policy matters than computerisation.

Besides record-keeping, the computer has been found a useful tool for time-table preparation, payroll preparation, classroom scheduling, accounting, budgeting, and monitoring of finances. The computer's capability for fast calculations, storage of information and manipulation of data can be optimally utilised to carry out these tasks.

Conclusion

As you can see, the application of computers in the role of a tool has a great potential in research, instructional presentations and administration. While most people will probably agree on the potential of the computer in the above areas, there are practical questions which could have to be dealt with before this potential is fully realised. These questions pertain to the selection of hardware (the computers and necessary peripherals), the software, preparation of a site, installation and maintenance of computers, and training of personnel to make effective use of the modern equipment and facility. As can be easily imagined, getting the right combination of the above would be paramount to effective utilisation of the potential of a computer. There are many low quality hardware and software products in the market and this calls for maximum caution when making the selections in these areas.

Computerisation is not an inexpensive process – it requires considerable financial and manpower investment. The returns on these investments can be high only if the initial investment is carefully planned and executed. Like any other tool, the benefits of computerisation will depend on whether we make a judicious use of its capabilities. It should be noted that computers are not magical boxes which will change overnight the working conditions and efficiency of our universities. There is most likely to be an adjustment phase beyond which the advantages of computerisation will start to come into evidence.

Universities which go in for computerisation will have to have a strong commitment for excellence in research, instruction and administration. In the Indian universities, there is a likelihood that computerisation will give rise to a plethora of emotions and thus, there will probably be a need to contend with some negative attitudes also. This, as is well known, is the fate of innovation and change.

I am firmly convinced that a well planned and careful implementation of the computer in the role of a tool or aid will have far reaching benefits in our universities.

REFERENCES

Merrill, P.F., Tolman, M.N., Christensen, L., Hammons, K., Vincent, B.R. and Reynolds, P.L. (1986). *Computers in Education,* Englewood Cliffs, NJ: Prentice-Hall.

Papert, S. (1980). *Mindstorms: Children, Computers and Powerful Ideas,* New York, Basic Books.

Taylor, R.P. (Ed.) (1980). *The Computer in the School: Tutor, Tool, Tutee*, New York: Teachers College Press.

7

EDUCATING THROUGH COMPUTERS: Methodology and Impact

RATNA GHOSH

> *The computer is the Proteus of machines. Its essence is its universality, its power to simulate. Because it can take on a thousand forms and can serve a thousand functions, it can appeal to a thousand tastes.*
>
> Seymour Papert, *Mindstorms*

The computer revolution in the West is transforming society at an alarming rate. By pervading the knowledge scene, it is also transforming the education systems. It is changing the content of education, the socio-cultural milieu within which the schools function and the nature of the learning process. The micro-computer revolution in the educational system has no precedence in educational history for its rate and scope of expansion. Seen as a mechanism for both multiplying the human intellect beyond past conceptions of the possible and extending it in time and space, the micro-computer has tremendous implications for education.

The rapid expansion in the use of micro-computers in schools has been viewed between variations of two extremes: that of naive optimism as a magic device, or naive pessimism as a fad or another expensive audio-visual aid. Both views derive from two basic assumptions:

(1) that the computer is primarily a passive delivery system for automated teaching of the standard curriculum, and
(2) that teaching with the computer does *not* involve fundamentally new ideas or techniques.

A completely different viewpoint is to see the computer as an active partner in the learning process which may be most effective in teaching things either not taught at all presently in schools, or not taught well. It is a technology or tool whose effectiveness is dependent on a complex interaction between it and the student. Unfortunately, as yet, very little is known about the nature of this interactive process. However, students of all ages can learn to use a computer at a level that is meaningful to them.

This paper has two sections. The first section looks briefly at specific applications of the computer in classrooms – the computer as used for instruction. The second section discusses the social impact of computers in the educational environment, specifically on students – computers as the technology of instruction.

Instructional Use of Computers

What kinds of problems can paper and pencils or books help solve? If you were to be asked that question, you would probably answer "every type of intellectual problem one can encounter". Like paper and pencil, the computer system is an interactive medium. Like books it stores material. In addition, it can automatically and rapidly follow directions involving the input, storage, manipulation and output of symbols. As a learning tool, an aid to problem-solving and for intellectual amplification, its power is tremendous.

The overall field of teaching and learning with the use of computers is referred to as computer-assisted learning (CAL). Substantial research over the past 20-25 years provides growing evidence that students learn more, better and faster with the computer's assistance.

CAL is divided into two major categories. In the tutor mode (Taylor, 1980) CAL, a computer, functions somewhat like a traditional teacher, presenting information, drilling and testing students, and maintaining records. This is usually called computer-assisted instruction or CAI. In the *tutee* mode CAL, the student, is in charge, directing the computer to carry out functions and by writing programs.

The Computer as Tutor: The nature of an application is not determined by the computer itself. Rather, it is determined by the software which produces the learning environment. The scope of software is constantly expanding and mass proliferation of educational software packages has caused problems of quality while offering variety. The application of programs ranges from pre-school children (e.g. number, letter, and colour recognition, and concepts in spatial relations) through all levels of school to post-graduate training. In the tutor mode, the software acts upon the student because it is a computer simulation of certain aspects of the teaching/learning process. Programs have moved from the dull routine drill-and-practice paradigm to tutorials and simulation which are interesting and emphasize conceptual thought and the development of problem-solving strategies. Good tutor mode embodies what is known about learning theory and the effects on mathematical (Supper, 1980) and science learning (Bork, 1980; Simon, 1983) are well documented. In addition to skill, factual and conceptual development, software is available for diagnostic subroutine which analyzes error patterns and provides remedial packages with graphics and/or voice synthesizers.

An important aspect of CAL is its individualization by which instruction is tailored towards the most effective learning. By incorporating computer graphics, individual instruction provides a highly motivated learning environment. Ideally, students at all grades must experience tutor mode CAL in a variety of disciplines so that they use drill and practice, tutorials and simulations in art, music, matter, science, language arts, social studies, etc. The responsibility for learning can be placed more explicitly on the student.

The Computer as Tutee: In the tutee mode, the student assumes the role of the teacher because the computer becomes the tutee. The child programs the computer. Programming a computer means communicating to it in a language both can understand. Papert points out that learning to communicate with a computer may change the way other learning takes place. The child, even at the pre-school age, is in control. Programming, interestingly, requires the child to think about the processes involved in learning. The very process of learning is transformed because it is active and self-directed. With the use of computer programming – BASIC, Logo, Pascal, Fortran, Smalltalk, Lisp languages – the student acquires greater and more sophisticated information – processing skills. The development of cognitive thinking strategies is facilitated, as well as abstract thinking, logical thinking, combinational and self-referential thought and problem-solving skills. As an aid to problem solving, the computer will substantially change the curriculum, especially in maths and sciences. Much attention has been given recently to providing a Logo environment for children, as a computer language both simple and powerful, based on Piaget's developmental theories. Seymour Papert (1980) who was involved in developing it, conceives of Logo as an environment in which children learn by doing and by thinking about what was done, continuously exploring the possibilities. By enabling the child to take the abstract and make it concrete, Logo is a powerful mediator in facilitating the child's conceptual processes.

The Computer as Tool: The computer is also used as a tool in regular classes, as well as in handicapped and learning disabled classes. The heavy uses of computer as a tool has been widely advocated (Bork, 1980; Papert, 1980) and the use of word processing packages, and statistical packages facilitates the activity involved.

Social Impact

> I believe that the computer presence will enable us to so modify the learning environment outside the classrooms that much if not all the knowledge schools presently try to teach with such pain and expense and such limited success will be learned, as the child learns to talk, painlessly, successfully, and without organized instruction. This obviously implies that schools as we know them today will have no place in the future. But it is an open question whether they will adapt by transforming themselves into something new or wither away and be replaced.
>
> (Papert, 1980:9)

Several educators have written about the revolutionizing effect of computers in education. If schools are not heading towards replacement, then radical change in our entire teaching and learning methods is predicted. Several humanist writers (Goodlad, 1979; Mumford, 1970) have difficulty coming to terms with the value of technology in the classroom because they see the machine as displacing human function totally. The computer is feared to mechanize, routinize, and depersonalize education by curbing the spontaneity, uniqueness and spirit of the student. Because a powerful machine like the computer has the capacity to be pervasive, there is an inherent danger. But what is inherent is not necessarily inevitable. It is important to keep in mind that the computer's pervasiveness is not guaranteed by its mere presence.

> In many schools today, the phrase "computer-aided instruction" means making the computer teach the child. One might say the *computer is being used to program* the child. In my vision, *the child programs the computer* and, in doing so, both acquires a sense of mastery over a piece of the most modern and powerful technology and establishes an intimate contact with some of the deepest ideas from science, from mathematics, and from the art of intellectual model building.
>
> (Papert, 1980:5)

Papert's idea of learner control of computer rather than program control of the learner is critical.

For this the teacher's knowledge is crucial. And because students vary in their readiness, responsibility in optimizing conditions for each learner means close involvement by the teacher. Unfortunately, most teachers, even today, are not computer literate within their own teaching areas and do not know how computers can help solve problems. The educational system will face a serious problem in that while computer systems will become increasingly capable aids to problem-solving, the computer knowledge of most teachers will lag far behind.

From the humanistic perspective, computers can promote human potential by enhancing options within the school. In his insightful article "The Computer as a Humanizing Influence in Education", Barger (1982), makes some significant observations. Computer literacy involves access to a network of information:

(1) The key is access because in this society what you "know" is what you can access. "An ignorance of the computer and its use may soon mean sacrifice of human *autonomy*" (p. 95).
(2) The *individuality* aspect is stressed. Its flexibility as a teaching instrument permitting different rates of learning have great value for all learners, and has demonstrated great success with retarded people.
(3) The computer amplifies thinking and doing, thus enhancing *rationality*.
(4) Because of the motivating power of the computer and potential for producing confidence by removing the fear of failure (object-to-think-with rather than black and white categories of right and wrong), it has great affective power.

(5) The *responsiveness* of the computer must not be underestimated. By providing a dialogical base it gives an opportunity to those students who do not normally engage in any type of dialogue.

Virtually all studies that look beyond cognitive development find significant positive changes in student attitudes (Fisher, 1984). Students feel more positive about themselves and school after being exposed to computers. These attitude changes tend to transfer into measureable behaviour changes. Increases in attendance, decreases in vandalism as at least a partial consequence of the introduction of computers have been reported. Lack of discipline problems and punctuality in CAL classes have also been observed, though hard research is lacking. While such reports suggest trends, some research is available on student interaction. Students tend to interact significantly differently, qualitatively and quantitatively, when working on the computer in groups. They become more cooperative and produce a collaborative environment.

Does the computer attract girls and boys equally? Gender differentiation is a product of social construction and the computer world is no different. Girls are under-represented among computer users in all grades, but this trend becomes more dramatic at higher levels. Girls predominate in word processing classes, boys in programming classes. Several surveys have established this without a doubt, but research is needed on why and what intervention strategies would be effective to change this unequal participation. Turkle (1984) points out that the styles of approach to the computer are different between boys and girls. Boys have "hard mastery", the mastery of the planner; girls have "soft mastery", the mastery of the artist.

There is general agreement that computers can have a powerful influence on how people think. How this can be turned in positive directions needs to be explored. Concern has been expressed by many about the present misuse of computers in schools which needs to undergo major change. As Papert points out, what *is* happening now is an empirical question, what *can* happen is a technical question, but *what* will happen is a political question, depending on social choices.

While the computer is not a culture in itself, it advances a very different cultural and philosophical outlook. Critics are apprehensive that computers might lead to less human association resulting in social fragmentation and even exacerbate class distinctions. Potential mental health hazards are worrying. No technology is without its side effects. Care must be taken to control and monitor use. Computers do humanize learning by permitting more personal, less alienating relationships with knowledge, and between fellow students and teachers. After all, the advantages are derived not from high technology but from the new possibilities for learning, thinking and growing emotionally and cognitively. The focus is not the machine but the mind. The computer must not be seen as a piece of hardware, but rather, as a communication tool, a telescope for the mind. We must look through it, not at it (Cartwright, 1983).

REFERENCES

Barger, R. (1982). The computer as a humanizing influence in education. *The Journal,* May, pp. 95-105.

Bork, A. 1980). Interactive learning. In R. Taylor (Ed.), *The Computer in the School: Tutor, Tool, Tutee*, New York: Teachers College Press.

Cartwright, G.F. (1983). Computers, Mind and Cosmos. Invited keynote address, First Annual McGill Computers in Education Conference, Montreal, McGill University.

Goodlad, J. (1979). *What Schools Are For*, Columbus, Ott: Phi Delta Kappa Educational Foundation.

Fisher, G. (1984). The social effects of computers in education. *Electronic Learning.* March.

Mumford, L. (1970). *The Myth of the Machine: The Pentagon of Power*. New York: Harcourt, Brace and World.

Papert, S. (1980). *Mindstorms*. New York: Basic Books.

Simon, S. (1983). Unprintable physics. *The Computing Teacher,* 10(7), pp. 14-16.

Supper, P. (1980). The teacher and computer assisted instruction. In R. Taylor (Ed.), *The Computer in the School: Tutor, Tool, Tutee.* New York: Teachers College Press.

Taylor, R. (Ed.) (1980). *The Computer in the School: Tutor, Tool, Tutee*. New York: Teachers College Press.

Turkle, S. (1984). *The Second Self: Computers and the Human Spirit.* New York: Simon and Schuster.

8

COMPUTER LITERACY AND BEYOND

WILLIAM A. STAHL

Where is the Life we have lost in living?
Where is the Wisdom we have lost in knowledge?
Where is the Knowledge we have lost in information?

— T.S. Eliot, *Choruses from "The Rock"*

What is vaguely put is poorly thought.

— Theodore Adorno, *Negative Dialectics*

Computer literacy is an idea whose time has come and already gone. The invention of the microcomputer in 1975, and its successful marketing by Apple in 1977, made the idea of "personal computing" possible. Once restricted by size and cost to the largest institutions, computers now became affordable to millions of people in North America. Egged on by speculations of best-selling futurologists such as Toffler (1980) and Naisbitt (1982) and hyped by computer industry advertising, people rushed to buy. The microcomputer became a fad. Educators were caught up in the fad too. The idea that schools and universities should teach "computer literacy" was eagerly pushed by computer enthusiasts and exploited by an industry on the lookout for a new market. Computer literacy was equated with basic skills such as reading and writing, and it was confidently declared: "It is rapidly becoming unthinkable that school children not have access to computers" (Moursund, 1983: 4).

The fad was short lived. Today, what Daniel Bell (1986) called the "initial gee-whiz optimism" about computers is nearly over. The computer industry is slumping, home computer sales are off, and many companies have failed. Personal computing magazines, which numbered over 50 in the early 1980s, have declined to a small handful, while the large, well-stocked computer sections in most bookstores have dwindled to a short shelf. Enrolment in university computer science classes is declining across Canada (Bowen, 1986) and the United States ("Fewer Students", 1987). Among educators, the debate over "computer literacy" is rapidly trailing off. The volume (if not the quality) of that debate can be measured by the number of articles published in any given year. The number of citations for "computer literacy" in the ERIC (Educational Resources Informational Centre) database describe a steep but short curve (see Table 8.1, Figure 8.1). The volume of writing seems to parallel the volume of sales.

TABLE 8.1 : Number of articles using "computer literacy" in index or title in ERIC

1974	1
1975	0
1976	2
1977	3
1978	14
1979	1
1980	17
1981	50
1982	211
1983	390
1984	358
1985	256
1986	91
Total	1394

But if the computer fad is over, the machines are still here. As educators, we are now faced with the less glamorous, but more serious and difficult, task of assessment. We need to re-examine the concept of "computer literacy". If we find its assumptions questionable – as I think they are – we are then compelled to lay out a new agenda for the role of computers in education.

Computer literacy is an idea which is "vaguely put". In spite of the massive debate, no clear consensus ever emerged on what the term means. Some definitions were extremely general, such as that offered by the U.S. Office of Technology Assessment: The ability of individuals to use an information system to help them at home and work" (1982: 19). Others were detailed lists of skills, knowledge, and attitudes (e.g. Charp, *et al.*, 1982: 6). Many narrowly focused on computers, emphasizing programming skills (e.g. Lindelow, 1983) while others placed broader emphasis upon such things as "information handling" (e.g. Seidel, 1982: 25). Much of the debate focused on whether computer literacy involved "awareness" of computers or "hands-on" experience, or how much of each. David Moursund offered what may be one of the better definitions:

> All students should become computer literate. This means that they should gain a substantial level of computer awareness and develop a functional level of skill in using computers as an aid to problem solving in a variety of disciplines (1983: 38).

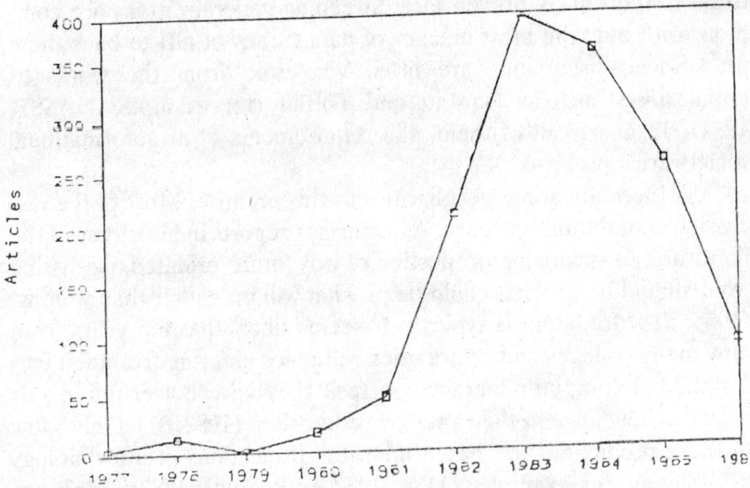

FIG 8.1: Citation of "computer literacy," ERIC

There was also considerable discussion about who should become computer literate. Some would restrict it to university or high school, but many more followed Moursund in arguing for all students, beginning in the earliest primary grades.

But why should all students become computer literate? Underlying all these definitions is an interconnecting series of assumptions which pyramid one upon the other to reach this conclusion. Yet throughout most of the debate the soundness of these assumptions is unquestioned.

The first assumption underlying the concept of computer literacy is that we are witnessing the emergence of a *qualitatively* new type of social order – information society. It is believed that "the computer will restructure society as completely as the steam engine did in a former age – and public education will not be spared" (Lindelow, 1983: 4). Because of this, "a computer-literate populace is as necessary to an information society as raw materials and energy are to an industrial society" (Deringer and Molnar, 1982: 3). These ideas are not unique. The work of Drucker (1968), Bell (1973), Masuda (1980), and others has provoked considerable discussion about "post-industrial" or "information" society. But most of the debate over computer literacy does not approach information society as an hypothesis to be tested but as proven fact. Sweeping generalizations are common, with only the most meager of data (if any at all) to back them up. Some discussions are lifted wholesale from the works of popularizers such as Naisbitt and Toffler (for example, NASSP, 1984). In nearly all of them, the requirements of an informational society are a premise.

Yet there are some peculiarities to this premise. Most of the discussion is in the future tense. As Danziger reports in his survey of the literature; "a surprising proportion of it is future-oriented, discussing what should be or what could be or what will be, rather than what is" (1985: 7). Moursund is typical: "It seems likely that ten years from now many colleges and universities will place entering freshmen into a remedial computer literacy course if they have not acquired this level of knowledge in their previous education" (1982: 81). Only a few of these predictions are based upon the projections of a technology assessment (for example, OTA, 1982 or Pogrow, 1983). Most are pure speculation.

Furthermore, many in this discussion display a peculiar attitude. While some speak optimistically, or with vision, or express the notion that "being a change agent can be fun" (Moursund, 1983: 46), for many more there is a strong undercurrent of fear. Many are afraid we won't "be ready" for an information society, that we will be left behind by the new technologies, that we will be rendered obsolete and unemployable. Charp *et al.* (1982) are typical in their worries that "the individual who does not have a grasp of these devices can be severely handicapped" (p. 1) and that "schools as we know them today may have no place in the future" (p. 25). Some have greater fears. According to Deringer and Molnar:

> Due to the decline in national productivity, the increase in foreign trade competition, and national defense and safety needs . . . the shortage of computer specialists and knowledge workers has raised the problem of computer literacy to the level of a national crisis (1982: 4).

Pogrow (1983) is even more dramatic. He argues that unless schools and universities make immediate, radical changes, they could suffer "environmental collapse" as the public abandons them for other institutions more in tune with the new technologies. This combination of vision and fear of the future is perhaps best illustrated by the U.S. National Association of Secondary School Principals (1984). They go on for pages describing the information society and all the new "high tech" jobs that students will need to be trained for. They talk about the "higher level of cognitivie skills" needed for "individual productivity and satisfaction" (p. 18). But then they note that the same projections say there will be relatively few of these jobs.

> By 1990, only 7 per cent of the workforce will be employed in the very highly technical jobs; five out of six workers, however, will be in clerical and service jobs such as waiters, waitresses, salespeople, janitors, security gurads, cashiers, and cooks (p. 17).

Their "vision of the future" is one of savage competition for the few places in the technological elite. The losers in this struggle will have nothing to look forward to but low skill, low-pay status, dead-end jobs. With such a vision as a basic premise of the computer literacy debate, is it any wonder it is so often underlaid with fear?

I think the reason why fear undergirds so much of this discussion can be found in a second assumption: technological determinism. Technology is seen as the driving force of social change, and computers are seen as *THE* decisive technology. Klassen and Anderson are typical of much of this debate: "There is little doubt, it seems, that life in the United States and the rest of the industrial world, and eventually all over the planet, will be incalculably changed by computer technology" (1982: 26). Notice the assumptions. The computer is the motor of change. "Progress" is linear, beginning in the most technologically "advanced" countries and spreading inexorably outward to the whole planet. And this "progress" will "impact" every aspect of our lives (by implication, whether we want it to or not). Thus the dilemma: "The microcomputer revolution is upon us. Almost every facet of our lives is impacted by the power of computers.... As educators what can we do?" (Brombacher, 1982: 5). Since the information society is seen as the inevitable consequence of the new technology, we have to "adjust", "adapt", and "get ready for it", If not, we will be left behind. Discussion of whether their vision of the information society is *good* or not is notably absent. After all, how can one morally evaluate the inevitability of progress? On those occasions when "values" are discussed, the emphasis is on "developing positive attitudes toward personal use of computers" (Klassen and Anderson, 1982: 31). The machine is dominant.

This technological determinism leads directly to a third assumption underlying the concept of computer literacy: that computers will transform teaching. It is in discussing teaching and the "technologically relevant curriculum" (Pogrow, 1983) that computer literacy enthusiasts become the most utopian. Technology is the way to " 'fix up' our schools" (NASSP, 1984: 1). Lindelow is representative:

> CAI (computer-assisted instruction) will free the classroom teacher to give individualized attention to students who need it and to concentrate on the "creative" aspects of teaching. Going back to the traditional method of teaching will become inconceivable. Computers will become – or will seem to become – indispensable to a good educational program (1983: 8).

All sorts of confident predictions are made, but when examined they prove surprisingly vague. The "creative" aspects of teaching are not specified. This is doubly vague since the accumulated experience of the teaching profession "will become inconceivable" once the machines come into their own. It is assumed that appropriate software will be developed, and that enough machines will be available in every classroom to permit "individualized attention". So far, these predictions have not come true. In spite of a huge potential market, little quality educational software has been written. According to the Minnesotta Educational Computing Corporation, only about 200 of 10,000 available educational programs are of any value (cited in Roszak, 1986: 51). And as Howlet reports, "of 3,000 software packages evaluated by the Alberta Department of Education over the past three years, only 300 have been recommended for use in the school's curriculum" (1986: 86). Most of the quality software which is available is machine-time intensive (Roszak, 1986; Bork, 1987) requiring very low student-machine ratios to be used effectively. According to a recent survey (Becker, 1987), in practice the "hands-on" implementation of computer literacy has most often meant word processing, drill-and-practice, simulation, and programing, usually in BASIC. But these are hardly revolutionary. According to Seymour A. Papert "drill-and-practice, simulation, and simple programming languages articulate the dominant structures of the traditional model for education and the dominant forms of educational practice" (1979: 74). They simply reinforce all the routine, all the rote-learning, and all the over-simplifications which the computer literacy enthusiasts claim would become a thing of the past. Becker concludes that "computers so far have had only limited impact on children's learning in school" (1987: 162).

More ominously, once a substantial investment is made in computers, pressures mount to use them, whether quality software is available or not. David Moursund recommends:

> All aspects of the curriculum should be reconsidered in light of the existence and widespread availability of calculators and computers. Modifications should be made to take into consideration the capabilities and applications of these machines (1983: 38).

In effect he is saying that using machines is what is most important and not the content of the class. If computers cannot perform to the standards of the traditional curriculum, lower the standards to the level of the machine. Only great faith in the efficacy of computers could lead even an enthusiast to make such a recommendation.

Why do so many of the computer literacy enthusiasts have so much faith in the machine? I think the answer lies in the fourth assumption, that data processing provides a model of thought. Computers are believed to be effective in teaching because they are like the human mind. The literature is studded with anthropomorphisms. Computers are said to have memories. We talk to them. We research artificial intelligence. Some claim that "communication with computers via computer language is analogous to interpersonal communication via ordinary language" (Klassen and Anderson, 1982: 28-29). Others even speak of "understanding the psychology of human/computer interactions" (Watt, 1982: 61). The conclusion is that "as the eighties progress, teaching computers will start acting more and more like the human teachers they are modelled after" (Lindelow, 1983. p. 18). Sometimes the roles are reversed, and humans are described in machine terms (Cf. Hunter, 1982: 33). Either way, a particular philosophy is being pushed.

This philosophy is most revealed in discussions of how computers aid in "problem solving".

> Problem solving is a central and unifying theme in education. Any discipline can be framed as a hierarchical set of problems to be solved. Instruction in a discipline leads to understanding the nature of the discipline's problems: the problems that have been solved, how to solve some of the problems that have been solved, what problems have not been solved, and how to formulate and attack new problems (Moursund, 1982: 77).

In other words, education is a process of learning algorithms. Once the correct algorithm has been selected or derived, the "solution" to any problem is then a matter of processing sufficient information (i.e. facts). At this point some disagreements arise. Some place a more positivistic emphasis on "the nature of the information we are required to process in order to understand our world", seeing changes occurring through "a consolidation and quantum jump in the database" (Seidel, 1982: 31). Others place more emphasis upon "procedural knowledge", usually described in terms of "acquiring skills" (Cf. Papert, 1980: 125). Both, however, understand thought and learning as directly analogous in human and computer. But, as Theodore Roszak (1986) argues, the data processing model of the mind is fundamentally flawed. People do not think with algorithms. Nor, in spite of the positivist's claims, does data determine our ideas. Indeed, our perceptions and intuitions – our ideas – shape the data.

> It is only when we strike a clear distinction between ideas and information that we can recognize that these are radically different levels of discourse requiring different levels of evaluation.... The ideas that govern the data are not information; nor are they sacrosanct matters of mathematical logic. They are philosophical

> commitments, the outgrowth of experience, insight, metaphysical conviction, which must be assessed as wise or foolish, childlike or mature, realistic or fantastic, moral or wicked.... Weighing such matters up in the critical scales requires an education which standard computer literacy will never provide (119-120).

Computer literacy assumes an epistemology, but it is one that must be questioned.

Thus we can see why the computer literacy enthusiasts have so much faith in the machine. If, as they assume, computer data processing is analogous to human thought; and if this technology is the motor force of social change; then, of course, computers will transform both the nature of teaching and the nature of society itself. These four assumptions lead to the conclusion that all students should become computer literate, and that computers should become the centerpiece of the curriculum. It is these assumptions which lead to the belief that computers are machines unlike any other. After all, automobiles, typewriters, and televisions have all found their niche in the schools, but few would advocate we rebuild *education* around them. These assumptions perhaps also account for much of the tone of the debate, the mixture of zeal and fear, earnestness and condescension that so characterizes the discussion. But if we *question* these assumptions instead of accepting them as premises – as I think we must – then most of the arguments for computer literacy evaporate.

How then can we assess the role of computers in education? If the computer literacy fad has provided inadequate answers, perhaps we can still learn from the debate. If the assumptions behind computer literacy are treated as questions, they may form the basis of an agenda for further research. In particular, I think there are three issues which we educators must address. All three questions involve the nature of structural change. Few social scientists today would dispute that the world economy has been undergoing structural change. But how significant are these changes, and how will they affect society?

The first issue this raises is what social role should the universities and schools play? In industrial society, education has usually functioned to train and discipline the labour force and to provide replacements for the ruling elite. Will (and should) that change? When computer literacy enthusiasts speak of information society, they are talking about a lot more than occupational mobility. They see a cultural transformation of the same order or magnitude as the industrial revolution. Information society is not only post-industrial, it is post-modern. If this analysis is correct, the nature and function of the universities and schools must and will be altered. "Accepting this transformation will consitute a Copernican revolution for pedagogy" (Nora and Minc, 1980: 132). A post-modern culture will require different values, and the very concepts of work, leisure, and education will need to be redefined.

But what if the analysis isn't correct? Are we even in fact moving into an information society? Certainly many of the claims made by the more utopian visionaries have not come to pass. Indeed, far from being a cultural revolution comparable to the industrial revolution, some say that "we should expect to see the effect of new technology in the next 20 years as an intensification of existing tendencies, and their expansion to new areas" (Rosenbrock, 1985: 641). Structural change does not necessarily mean profound cultural change. Instead of post-modern, information society may be hyper-modern – faster, more intense, but not fundamentally different in essence from industrial society.

Our first task, then, is technology assessment. We have to monitor and understand the nature and direction of the changes in our society, and find the appropriate role for our educational institutions.

A second issue is the nature of education itself. What do computers mean for how we do our work, and particularly for our self-education? With their data processing model of thought, the computer literacy enthusiasts claim that all aspects of education within the university and school must and will be transformed. Others claim that computers are, in Joseph Weizenbaum's phrase, "a solution looking for problems" (1985: 89) and that their effect on education will be no more than that of television. Perhaps a concrete example will illuminate some of the ramifications.

Whatever the status of information society, the "information explosion" is here already. For example, the ERIC database records 1394 articles, in English only, on the topic of "computer literacy" (see Table I). Let us assume all of them are immediately available. Let us also assume that it takes on average two hours to read each of them. If I read for 8 hours a day, 5 days a week, for 50 weeks a year, it would take me 1.39 years *just to get "caught up"*. This, of course, assumes that I am doing *nothing else* but reading articles.

What does this mean for education? First, it casts doubt on claims that our real need is more information, more accurately and more quickly. We have too much information. No one can handle the amount of data computers can give us now. What *is* important, on the other hand, is one's ability to select and interpret, to find what is important amidst all the "noise". Such skills go beyond our narrow, departmentally limited conceptions of knowledge. (Dare we call it wisdom?) But perhaps a person with these skills may be the basis of real value in our changing economy (Cf. Cohen and Shannon, 1984). Thus our second task is to discover how we can develop such people, and the role computers will play in educating them.

The third issue is that of control and decision-making. It is the question of power. This isn't an important issue for computer literacy enthusiasts. Since most of them see technology determining social change, control and decision-making are not problematical for them. Technological "progress" is inevitable. But if we question technological determinism, power becomes *the* problem. As Gale Moore writes: "An understanding of changes in the distribution of power and control are of central importance to an understanding of the nature of the change occurring in advanced industrial economies" (1986: 11-12). In order to discover the social impact of computers, we are forced to ask who in fact does make decisions and exercises control. How are resources in our educational institutions allocated, and with what criteria? Who decides what technologies will be adopted, and how they will be used? Who controls access? Arnold Pacey (1983) observes:

> If we are to have a democratic control over technological development, we need public inquiry and technology assessment procedures that are able to strip off the various disguises which allow fundamental conflicts of basic values and political interests to hide behind utilitarian arguments about benefits and costs (157).

We should not underestimate the difficulty in doing this. He concludes: "It is easy to see why such issues are so rarely fully debated. To engage in a genuinely open dialogue is inevitably to share the final decision" (p. 157). Technology assessment has often encountered resistance from decision-makers. But only if we directly confront the issue of power and control can we hope to answer the other questions either.

The computer literacy fad has come and gone. But computers are here, and the structural changes in the economy associated with them continue. Now that the enthusiasts have had their day, our task is to go beyond computer literacy to the more difficult job of assessment.

REFERENCES

Becker, Henry Jay (1987). "Using Computers in Instruction", *Byte*, Vol. 12, No. 2, February.

Bell, Daniel (1973). *The Coming of Post-Industrial Society*, New York: Basic Books.

Bell, Daniel (1986). "Address to the World Congress on Education and Technology", Vancouver, B.C., 22 May.

Bork, Alfred (1987). "The Potential for Interactive Technology", *Byte,* Vol. 12, No. 2, February.

Bowen, Beverly (1986). "Out Modemed: Computer Science Enrolment Falling Fast", *The Globe and Mail,* 2 August.

Brombacher, Bruce E. (1982). Forward, In Kepner, Henry S. (Ed.), *Computers in the Classroom*, Washington, D.C.: National Education Association.

Charp, Sylvia *et al.* (1982). *Layman's Guide to the Use of Computers in Education,* Washington, D.C.: The Association for Educational Data Systems.

Cohen, Dian and Shannon, Kristin (1984). *The Next Canadian Economy,* Montreal: Eden Press.

Danziger, James N. (1985). "Social Science and the Social Impacts of Computer Technology", *Social Science Quarterly,* Vol. 66, No. 1, March.

Deringer, Dorothy and Molnar, Andrew (1982). Key Components for a National Computer Literacy Program, In Seidel, Robert J., Anderson, Ronald E. and Hunter, Beverly (Eds.), *Computer Literacy,* Orlando, Floria: Academic Press Inc.

Drucker, Peter (1968). *The Age of Discontinuity*, New York: Harper & Row.

"Fewer Students Study Computers" (1987). *The Globe and Mail*, 21 January.

Howlett, Karen (1986). "Can Our Kids Hack It With Computers?", *Report on Business,* Vol. 3, No. 5, November.

Hunter, Beverly (1982). Computer Literacy: 1949-1979, In Seidel, Robert J., Anderson, Ronald E. and Hunter, Beverly (Eds.), *Computer Literacy*, Orlando, Florida: Academic Press Inc.

Klassen, Daniel L. and Anderson, Ronald E. (1982). Computer Literacy, In Kepner, Henry S. (Ed.), *Computers in the Classroom,* Washington, D.C.: National Education Association.

Lindelow, John (1983). *Administrator's Guide to Computers in the Classroom,* Eugene, Oregon: Clearinghouse for Educational Management, University of Oregon.

Masuda, Yoneji (1980). *The Information Society*, Washington, D.C.: World Future Society.

Moore, Gale (1986). "Post-Industrialism: An Analytical Model Towards the Study of Social Control". Paper presented at the annual meetings of the Canadian Sociology and Anthropolgy Association, Winnipeg, Manitoba, 5 June.

Moursund, David (1982). Personal Computing for Elementary and Secondary School Students, In Seidel, Robert J., Anderson, Ronald E. and Hunter, Beverly (Eds.), *Computer Literacy,* Orlando, Florida: Academic Press Inc.

Moursund, David (1983). *School Administrator's Introduction to Instructional Use of Computers*, Eugene Oregon: International Council for Computers in Education.

Naisbitt, John (1982). *Megatrends,* New York: Warner Books.

National Association of Secondary School Principles (NASSP), (1984). *High Tech Schools,* Reston, Virginia: NASSP.

Nora, Simon and Minc, Alain (1980). *The Computerization of Society: A Report to the President of France,* Cambridge, Mass.: MIT Press.

Office of Technology Assesment (OTA) (1982). *Informational Technology and Its Impact on American Education,* Washington, D.C.: OTA.

Pacey, Arnold (1983). *The Culture of Technology,* Cambridge, Mass.: MIT Press.

Papert, Seymour A. (1979). Computers and Learning, In Detouzos, Michael and Moses, Joel (Eds.), *The Computer Age: A Twenty-Year View,* Cambridge, Mass.: MIT Press.

Papert, Seymour A. (1980). *Mindstorms,* New York: Basic Books.

Pogrow, Stanley (1983). *Education in the Computer Age,* Beverly Hills, California: Sage Publications.

Rosenbrock, Howard (1985). A New Industrial Revolution? In Forester, Tom (Ed.), *The Information Technology Revolution,* Cambridge, Mass.: MIT Press.

Roszak, Theodore (1986). *The Cult of Information,* New York Pantheon Books.

Seidel, Robert J. (1982). On the Development of an Information Handling Curriculum: Computer Literacy, A Dyunamic Concept, In Seidel, Robert J., Anderson, Ronald E. and Hunter, Beverly (Eds.), *Computer Literacy,* Orlando, Florida: Academic Press Inc.

Toffler, Alvin (1980). *The Third Wave,* New York: Bantham Books.

Watt, Daniel H. (1982). Education for Citizenship in a Computer-based Society, In Seidel, Robert J., Anderson, Ronald E. and Hunter, Beverly (Eds.), *Computer Literacy*, Orlando, Florida: Academic Press Inc.

Weizenbaum, Joseph (1985). The Myths of Artifical Intelligence, In Forester, Tom (Ed.), *The Information Technology Revolution*, Cambridge, Mass.: MIT Press.

9

WHERE IS TECHNOLOGY HEADED?

R.B. MAGUIRE

Any sufficiently advanced technology is indistinguishable from magic.

—Arthur C. Clarke

The often used phrase "the only constant in change" applies to the current fields of computing and communications more than probably any others in history. Rapidly changing technology and the related effects and potentials for higher education are simultaneously a blessing and a curse for the teacher or researcher who would utilise this technology. In this paper those technologies relevant to higher education are reviewed and the related problems and potentials are considered with the objective of identifying topics for future research.

Introduction

As educators and users of high technology, we know that there is a fundamental underlying trend that strongly influences our decisions to adopt high technology in education. That trend is the continuing and frequently dramatic decline in the cost of technology, particularly communications and computer technology (Moad, 1986: 26).

While computing professionals, directors of computer centres and the business community have planned for growth in light of this trend for many years, the major breakthrough in cost for most educators came with the advent of the microcomputer. The earliest microcomputers, based in the INTEL 8008 and 8080, were too limited in capacity and too technically demanding to make much impression in education. However, this situation began to change with the Apple II and Commodore PET microcomputers.

Since about 1980 we have been in the position of being able to purchase microcomputers for personal use or for use by small academic units. Prior to this point the majority of academics depended on the availability of computer facilities from a centralised organisation such as the university computer centre. The primary users of these facilities were those academics whose expertise included this technology, that is, the engineers, computer scientists and business school faculty. Other disciplines which did get involved with mainframe computing, including education departments with interest in CAI, grew comfortable with technology that changed only slowly over time. Mainframe computers were purchased with the intent that their lifetime would be many years. Moreover, when these central facilities were upgraded, a major concern was that existing applications should be upward compatible with the new machinery. IBM operating systems, for example, changed little from the mid-sixties through the seventies. When the University of Regina Academic Computing Department surveyed its academic users in 1983 about replacing the Xerox Sigma 9 used since 1973, the most common description entered under "desirable features" was that the new machine should resemble the old machine except be faster.

This situation was to change dramatically in the eighties. Marketing strategies that meant vendors would announce major hardware revisions only every five years disappeared with the movement of academics to microcomputer usage. The same trend that made inexpensive microcomputer facilities possible has left us in a continual state of flux. We know, for example, that new releases of microcomputers will be cheaper in six months or a year. We also know that the price-performance ratio will improve. Accompanying these hardware related changes will be software enhancements as applications are developed or modified to use the new capabilities of the hardware. Trade magazines dedicate almost as much space to speculation about the potential of the next release of this or that vendor's hardware or software as to the current product capabilities.

The general and observable reaction is a reticence to invest in today's technology knowing that tomorrow's offerings will reduce costs or, more importantly, provide new hardware and software features. The microcomputer market is characterised by a pervasive belief that delivery equates to obsolescence. Moreover, the technology enhancements we know will be available with the next model of machine or release of the applications package are typically real and measurable. Not only is our neighbour, colleague or competitor able to claim his model is better, he can demonstrate its improved speed or functionality. The marketing of consumer products such as automobiles, for example, depends on our desire to have a newer, fancier car than our neighbour. Yet we all know that the automotive industry moves at such a slow technological pace that our neighbour's new purchase is, at best, a marginal improvement over last year's offering. Most of the improvements will consist of styling changes. This is not true for microcomputer technology.

The result is the quandary we face in the application of high technology to education. In the main, the technologies applicable to education require significant investments of our time and energy to apply the technology. Good course material is difficult to develop regardless of the technology involved. There are numerous ancillary difficulties including the training or retraining of academics to use the technology, pedagogic suitability of the technology and release time to develop the material. Furthermore, rapid changes in technology mean that, even if we solve all these problems, our efforts are fated to obsolescence in a cruely short period of time. The software we write will require continual maintenance. The graphic material produced will not fit new expanded screen resolutions or it suffers in comparison to what our colleagues are now generating with the latest model. Some academics enjoy the pursuit of the latest technology. Others are frustrated at the need to engage in this chase and, unfortunately, others among us simply opt out.

Technologies for Higher Education

As background to further discussion of the potentials and pitfalls in the use of high technology consider those technologies of special relevance to education. That component of high technology with the greatest potential and correspondingly highest visibility is the microprocessor delivered in the form of a microcomputer. The microcomputer has transferred the development of applications from the hands of a few computing professionals to a vast array of academics, students, clerks and individuals with talents and interests that lead them far beyond the scope of the applications envisaged by the computing professionals.

On university and college campuses the microcomputer is moving closer to becoming all pervasive as students elect to purchase or are required to purchase their own microcomputers (*Time,* 1985: 80).

For example , at Philadelphia's Drexel University, the tuition is $9,000 plus $1,020 for an Apple Macintosh computer and software. Over 6,000 Macintoshes are already on campus. English professors refuse to accept essays that are not typed on a word processor. In order to encourage the integration of these microcomputers into the school's curriculum, Drexel has invested $2.8 million in faculty computer training. Faculty who proposed ideas for good educational computer programs were paired with student and professional programmers to see these ideas to completion. Excellent results are reported by history professors who put exercises and factual material onto the computer and now concentrate on classroom discussion of ideas rather than dates and details. Drexel is conducting a five-year study of the impact of the microcomputer on campus and the study includes a measure of intangibles such as self-confidence and optimism about the future amongst faculty and students, with current samples showing sharp increases.

The CPU capabilities of these systems are well beyond the mainframe computers of only a few short years ago (Moad, 1986: 26). From the INTEL 8080, 8088 and 8086 microprocessors there is now widespread use of the INTEL 80286 and Motorola 68000, 68010 and 68020. The new processor generations including the INTEL 80386 and Motorola 68030 will soon be available (Digital Design, 1986: 28, Scalees, 1986: 129). Accompanying the rapid spread of high speed processing power is a decline in the cost of memory. Machine configurations of 1-2 megabytes of memory are commonplace already. While Apple has not released a machine based on the 68020, nor IBM a machine using the 80386, smaller vendors are already providing a taste of the power of machines that will be the next generation of microcomputers. Figure 9.1 shows the performance of four upgrade packages for the Apple Macintosh that install 68020 processors and the Motorola 68881 floating point co-processor (Ushijima and Foster, 1986: 88). A Vax-11/780 performs from 800,000 Whetstones per second (one user on the machine) down to 200,000 Whetstones (15 user load). The Prodigy 4 does 500,000 Whetstones. Clearly Vax-11/780 level performance is now available in a microcomputer. IBM and Apple are expected to announce machines with this speed within the year.

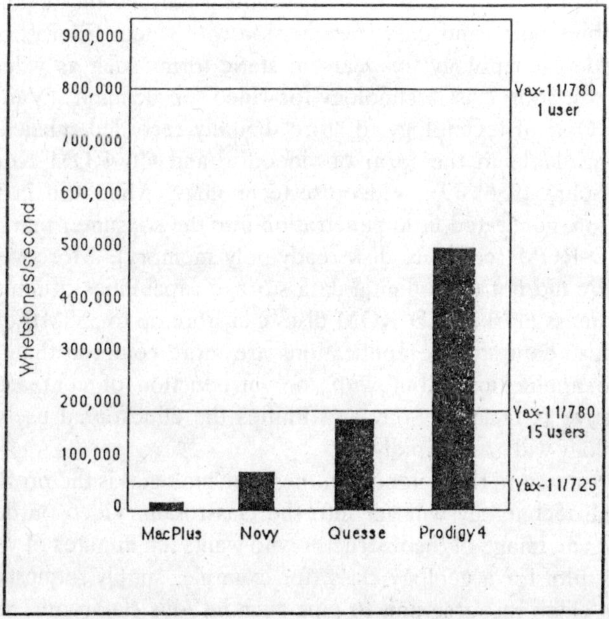

FIG 9.1: Whetstone benchmark of modified Mac Plus and Vax-11/780 with floating point co-processor

As this trend continues, the concerns of generations of data processing professionals over computing speed and memory capacity will disappear. Tomorrow's users of computer technology will consider central processing capacity and memory as almost a free resource and their ideas for educational applications will reflect this lack of constraint.

In place of memory and processor speed concerns, however, there is a new set of problems to confront. For example, the technology to create large local area networks that cover whole universities is available today. It is still relatively expensive and it is unclear how the application of this technology may affect our educational institutions. The applications that existed with time-shared computing systems are certainly going to be available in the networking of whole institutions.

There will continue to be electronic mail and centralised large databases as used now. However, the affiliated communications technologies of fibre optics and video switching portend the opportunity to combine voice and data transmission with video. Educators have used video technology for years in static forms such as videotape. There will soon exist technology for video "on demand" (Van Vlict, 1987). Optical technology to store digitally recorded images is already available in the form of videodisc and CD-ROM Kirchner, 1986; Sehr, 1986: 79). Videodisc technology, while still in use in education, generated little penetration into the consumer market unlike CD-ROM (compact disk ready-only memory). Moreover, the videodisc did not offer digital data storage capabilities of interest to the business market. CD-ROM discs can store up to 550MB of data. Presently, data storage applications are more common than image storage applications, but with the introduction of compact disc-interactive (CD-1) by Sony and Philips the educational use of this technology will grow rapidly.

In contrast to the potential of these technologies is the problem of how the technology will get into the classroom. Video on demand suggests an image of the instructor who wants ten minutes of volcanic activity film for a geology class, for example, simply requesting the central video resource unit to pipe such into his classroom. Such visions are exciting and make excellent justification for the need to implement high capacity networks on our campuses. However, insufficient attention is being paid to problems such as who collects this material and gets it onto CD-ROM, who does the cataloguing and especially how is the material displayed since most classrooms today have no more sophisticated audio/visual equipment than an overhead projector. Moreover, before we have had a chance to investigate CD-ROM technology, we have begun to hear about digital tape technology and what a technological marvel it will be when available over the next few years.

In addition to these hardware developments, there have been corresponding improvements to the software of the microcomputer systems. In particular, the user interface is changing rapidly with the availability of bit-mapped, high resolution screens. The user interface on the Apple Macintosh and software packages such as TOPVIEW (Byers, 247) is highly iconographic and attempts to minimize the learning period for the novice user. Naturally, unless you have kept pace with the latest hardware developments, none of this software is available to you.

Applications of the Technology

The application of educational technology by institutions varies from passive acknowledgement that the students themselves have often purchased microcomputers to exciting, institution wide commitments to the development and use of the latest technology. The two highest profile projects to date are in the United States and are the joint Carnegie-Mellon/IBM project Andrew (Morris and Satyanarayanan *et al.*, 1986: 284) and the Massachusetts Institute of Technology Athena project (Balkovich, Lenman, and Parmelec, 1986: 1214).

Andrew is the result of the formation in 1982 of the Information Technology Center (ITC), a joint venture between IBM and Carnegie-Mellon. The Andrew project is intended to affect and enhance university education by increasing dramatically the availability of computer-aided instruction materials, by creating new tools to improve teaching, by providing a communications system that will connect every member of the university community and by enabling better access to databases on and off campus.

The system is based on four key technologies: personal computers, faster graphics, high bandwidth networks and time-sharing file systems. Andrew is a good example of the designer's need to anticipate trends in hardware technology. In 1983 project management agreed that the network workstation would require a million-instructor-per-second processor, virtual memory, a megabyte of real memory and a local area network connection. It was anticipated correctly that such a machine would sell for $10,000 US by the mid-eighties. Furthermore, the project assumed that subsequent price reductions would make such a configuration affordable to students within the next few years. In essence, the project anticipated the convergence of the engineering workstation and the personal computer that we are just beginning to witness (Hoffmann, 1986: 56).

From the software perspective the most interesting feature of Andrew is the window manager that shares a bit-mapped display amongst several processes. The window manager is based on the Xerox Star (Smith Irby *et al.*, 1982) user interface. Its key traits are the pop-up menus, windows and mouse interface that have become commonplace in the personal computer marketplace. From the educational perspective, the Andrew implementors are designing a network wide file system and user interface that will provide numerous insights into the management and presentation of classroom material as the system evolves.

Project Athena at MIT is also exploring the potential application of high technology to the university curriculum. In contrast to the Andrew project, Athena has concentrated more on the use of available technology rather than on the design of a new workstation and network. Half of the Athena project budget of $20 million has gone to faculty members for the creation of new applications software to be integrated into the MIT curriculum. Almost all of MIT's academic departments are involved in an educational development project. An important element of this development is to design "virtual laboratory" enhancements to the experimental laboratory experience. In one application in biology an electron microscope is simulated by retrieving sequences of pictures from a database that make the image appear to enlarge or shrink. A similar submarine simulation uses 50,000 pictures to explore 20,000 feet beneath the Atlantic Ocean. For a Spanish lesson, you are transferred to Bogota, Columbia and set down in the middle of a detective mystery in which you partake speaking in Spanish. Exper-tutor software is being designed that will go beyond traditional CAI software by using expert system principles to lead the student through the subject material in the way a classroom teacher might.

An older large scale project that has the same scope and size as Andrew and Athena is the Plato Project (Smith and Sherwood, 1976) at the University of Illinois where over 10,000 hours of course work have been developed. Plato was developed by Control Data Corporation and used the earliest widely distributed educational workstation. Plato workstations are medium resolution graphics terminals with minimal intelligence that require attachment to a central CDC processor. These workstations were developed prior to the spread of microcomputers and were expensive. The CDC processor required to support more than a few workstations was also very expensive. However, Plato software is being converted to run on common microcomputers and costs are declining.

These projects are massive in size relative to the resources of a typical university. Andrew has over 150 person years of software development to date while the Athena budget is $20 million. The typical university is much more likely to take the approach of providing a central time-sharing facility and a limited number of microcomputers for faculty and students ((Frank and McLean, 1986: 12).

Even without the financial resources of MIT or CMU, there are possibilities for the application of technology in the classroom. The available central computing facilities will have electronic mail systems which range from the rudimentary to very elaborate systems which are integral components of office automation systems such as Digital Equipment's All in One or IBM's PROFS system. These systems provide much more than electronic mail. Lecture notes, assignments, exams and problems can be stored in these systems, catalogued, indexed and retrieved from semester to semester. Direct mailings to students can take seconds rather than hours of secretarial and faculty overhead. Any links to the institution's administrative systems are likely to be on mainframe machines. These links might offer fast distribution of student lists to faculty, administration of research account finances and other administrative support which is still best implemented on a larger system. The central time-shared system is also the most effective gateway for large numbers of faculty and students to use to public networks such as Usenet or Bitnet.

Unfortunately, microcomputer software for education is not likely to be available on the microcomputers provided by the institution. The organisation managing the micro facilities is unlikely to want the difficult and unfamiliar job of identifying such software. Mainframe software of use to the academic was probably purchased because of its utility in an administrative function. Thus, the collection of microcomputer software usually consists of a few language packages and those database or spreadsheet packages that dominate market sales in Fortune 500 companies. The academic is going to have to develop his own expertise in locating useful microcomputer applications. However, there are packages in the micro marketplace with potential and which do not exist on mainframe computers, so this search will have its rewards. For example, the latest exciting development in the microcomputer field is in desktop publishing (Macuser, 1986). While most publications, including new specialist magazines, covering this development have described applications in the office, the ease of combining text and graphics holds considerable potential for educators. Figure 9.2 is a humorous example of a graphic done with a micro drawing program which I use in class to illustrate the need for file backup.

FIG 9.2: MacPaint picture from INFO-Mac user group

With the financial and budgetary constraints on higher education today, it is imperative that technology take the academic in the direction of higher productivity. That is, the technology must eventually help us deal with larger classes, administrative overhead and limited research funding.

REFERENCES

Balkovich, E., Lerman, S. and Parmelee, R.P. (1985). Computing in Higher Education: The Athena Experience. *Communications of the ACM*. November, 1985, Vol. 28, No. 11, pp. 1214-1224.

Byers, T.J. TopView. *BYTE,* Vol. 10, No. 11, pp. 247-251.

Desktop Publishing on the Mac. Special supplement in MacUser. June, 1986.

Digital Design. Software vendors tout 80386 for All applications. November (1986), p. 28.

Digital Equipment Corporation. All-in-1 Office Menu Primer. AA-N320A-TE.

Frank, J.L. and McLean, E.R. (1986). Summary of the Second Annual UCLA Survey of Business School Computer Usage. *Communications of the ACM.* January, 1986, Vol. 29, No. 1, pp. 12-18.

Hoffmann, T.V. (1986). RT PC: A significant departure. *PC Tech Journal,* Vol. 4, No. 12. December, 1986, pp. 56-66.

IBM. Introducing the Professional Office System. GH20-6795.

Kirchner, G. (1986). Applications of interactive videodiscs in education. Presented at The World Congress on Education and Technology. Vancouver, May, 1986.

Moad, J. (1986). Too much ain't enough. *DATAMATION.* August 15, 1986, pp. 26-28.

Morris, J.H., Satyanarayanana, M., *et al.* (1986). Andrew: A Distributed Personal Computing Environment. *Communications of the ACM.* March, 1986, Vol. 29, No. 3, pp. 184-201.

Scales, H. (1986). MC68030 manages memory. *Digital Design.* September, 1986, pp. 129-131.

Sehr, B.K. (1986). High noon for CD-ROM. *DATAMATION.* November 1, 1986, pp. 79-88.

Smith, D.C. (1982). Irby, C., *et al.* The Star user interface: an overview. Proceedings of the National Computer Conference 1982.

Smith, S. and Sherwood, B.A. (1976). Educational uses of the PLATO computer system. *Science* 192.

Time Magazine (1985). A Machine on Every Desk. October 21, pp. 80-82.

Ushijima, D. and Foster, D.L. (1986). New ways to a faster Mac. *Macworld*, August 1986, pp. 88-94.

Van Vliet, P. (1987). Unpublished proposal for an intelligent building project at the University of Regina.

SECTION III

USE AND IMPACT OF COMPUTERS

10

TECHNOLOGY AND VALUES:
The Question of Assessment

WILLIAM A. STAHL

Rapid computer might be useful for something.

— Headline, *The Globe and Mail*

Social Life is essentially *practical*. All mysteries which mislead theory into mysticism find their solution in human practice and in the comprehension of this practice.

— Karl Marx, *VIII Thesis on Feuerbach*

We are living in the midst of a revolution, or so we are told. Nearly every film, TV broadcast and magazine demonstrates (or hypes) the "wonders" and "magic" of new technology. "High tech" has become the buzzword of corporations and governments. Professional seers rush to market with their visions of utopia or disaster. Enthusiasm for computers, or fear of them, seems to be the order of the day. But what is the reality behind the mystique of the computer? If we are to avoid getting caught up in the current wave of technological mysticism, we will have to deal with the question of assessment.

Before we begin, I should clarify the meaning of "technology" and "assessment". Technology is the knowledge, tools and procedures used in a society in order to get work done and achieve desired, practical ends. The emphasis here is on practical knowledge. Technology is more than machinery; it is before all a form of social organization. A factory is thus a better illustration of technology than the machines which are in it. Assessment is judgement and evaluation. It is the practical application of criteria and standards to make a decision as to the merit, value, appropriateness etc. of whatever is being assessed. Technology assessment (TA) was first developed in the United States in the late 1960s. It can be defined as "a class of policy studies which systematically examines the effects on society that may occur when a technology is introduced, extended, or modified with special emphasis on those consequences that are unintended, indirect, or delayed" (National Science Foundation, cited in: Boroush *et al.*, 1980: 43). It has been closely associated with government and corporate policymaking processes, primarily to enhance the benefits of new technological development and to avoid unforeseen or adverse impacts. Environmental impact assessment (EIA) and social impact assessment (SIA) are subdisciplines of technology assessment.

Technology assessment is a procedure which has not lived up to its potential. While there are a number of reasons for this (Cf. OECD, 1983; Slack, 1984), I contend that the key issue in the question of assessment is the question of values. It is in discourse on the relationship of technology and values that technology assessment has most displayed its weaknesses. Its problems have not been so much technical or methodological, but in establishing criteria, standards and evaluations. Only by understanding and interpreting such discourse and the assumptions which underlie it will we be able to judge the social impact of new technologies.

The question of the role of values has been fundamental to the assessment of technology. This is, of course, in part tautological. Since assessment means evaluation, values are part of the procedure by definition. Nevertheless, the role of values in assessment remains controversial. Why is this? I think the problems lie in the assumptions the practitioners of TA make in doing their work. What are these assumptions? While there are many, four are particularly relevant.

First, they tend to operate within a mechanical conception of cause and effect. Cause-effect relationships are seen in terms of discrete variables interacting in a linear, usually unidirectional manner. Since "independent" and "dependent" variables are isolated from their environemnt, their relationship is purely mechanical. That is, in the analysis of any given situation or point in time, variables are seen to interact as A-->B (A causes B). Introducing reciprocity, or a "feedback loop", (A<-->B) does nothing to alter the linearity and mechanical nature of the causal relationship. Thus "the underlying assumption in TA/EIA is that a technological intervention as a cause produces impacts as its effects. These impacts, in turn acting as causes, may produce other as (higher order) effects" (Porter *et al.*, 1980: 45). The language they use reflects this. The connection between technological innovation and its impact on society is compared variously to "the links of a chain" (Ogburn, 1957: 22), "the play on the billiard table (Ogburn, 1957: 20), or "a chain reaction of change" (Toffler, 1970: 32). A technical innovation is seen as having a direct or primary impact, which is usually the function it was intended to perform. Rippling out from this direct impact are a series of derivative, or secondary, effects which may in turn cause further derivative, or tertiary, effects, and so on. The more remote the effect from the original cause, the weaker its influence and the more likely that "several derivative causes may operate conjointly to produce an effect" (Ogburn, 1957: 21). Thus the causal relationship may become quite complex as one moves to more distant or higher order consequences.

Secondly, the mechanistic paradigm assumes that the goal of social science is to provide "a stock of law-like generalizations with strong predictive power" (MacIntyre, 1985: 88). In the literature, it is not uncommon to find statements such as Hornell Hart's formulation of a "sociological law" – "Over the long sweep of time, man's power to carry out his purposes has been increasing with steeper and steeper acceleration, but with stagnation and setbacks" (1957: 458). Even more common are graphs and diagrams predicting continual "progress" in technological development (Cf. Pacey, 1983). Throughout, a central assumption of TA is the goal of prediction. This is a logical extension of the mechanistic conception of causality. Comte's slogan *Savoir pour prevoir, prevoir pour pouvoir*" (Knowledge for prediction, prediction for power) (in Lowrance, 1985: 53) has set the agenda for generations of social scientists. The goal is mastery over society, in the same way that the natural sciences have given mastery over nature.

Thirdly, the form this "predictive power" takes is openly or tacitly deterministic. Some assume that "scientific research and technological innovation are basic determinants of economic and social change" (OECD, 1983: 7). They believe in technological determinism, or as E.G. Mesthene put it, "technological change induces or 'motors' social change" (1970: 26). Others see the determination running the other way. As Daniel Bell describes, technology "is embedded in a social support system, and it is the support system, not the technology, that determines its use. One can, with the same technology, design totally different outcomes by designing different support systems" (1979: 461). Yet others argue that "a relationship of mutual causality exists between technology and society. This complex relationship leads to the creation of background conditions, immediate or first order effects, and higher order effects" (Porter *et al.*, 1980: 23). Whichever way the causal relationship is seen to run though, the assumptions are those of a mechanical system, the operation of which can be understood and predicted. Prediction requires a determined future.

Fourthly, the natural sciences are assumed to be the model for the social sciences. The "scientific method" based upon induction, a sharp dichotomy between data and theory, subject and object, fact and value, and a strong emphasis upon the "objectivity" of results has been upheld as an ideal to be followed. (Difficulties in actually realizing this ideal are often attributed to the "immaturity" of the social sciences. As the social sciences "progress" and become more "mature", it is assumed they will become more like the natural sciences (Cf. Giddens, 1979 or Lowrance, 1985 on the antiquity of the social sciences).

This assumption creates problems for TA, especially in terms of the validity of its predictions and with values. According to Porter *et al.*, the validity "refers to being well grounded in fact and verifiable. In the case of research dealing with the future, we take validity to refer to the congruence between predicted and actual results" (1980: 45). Yet, they are forced to admit, predictions are always "uncertain". If this assumption makes verifiability a difficult issue, values are even more so. As a consequence, the OECD reports:

> After years of heated controversy, the meaning of the term [assessment] is still questioned, and its ambiguity remains far from being dispelled. From the start, evaluation of impacts has tended to be viewed as a process of rationalisation of hard and soft elements, trends and effects within which (for the sake of analysis) the value-free questions of "facts" can be separated from the value-laden questions of policy. In other terms, the underlying assumption – shared by some and doubted by others – is that a "neutral" scientific database can be distinguished from inferred probabilities, conditional conjectures and normative injunctions (1983: 49).

What is assumed to be "scientific" is incompatible with practical realities.

Are these assumptions valid? Do they offer a viable way of working through the questions of technology and values? I think the answer is no. Until technology assessment is better able to handle these questions, it won't be able to realize its potential. There are two problems here for technology assessment. First is the attempt to separate "scientific fact" from "value-laden policy". Second is an inadequate conception of values. In both these cases, over-reliance upon a mechanical paradigm of science (see Appendix) has frustrated assessment.

The first problem arises from the assumptions about verifiability and the necessity of separating fact from value. Instead of trying to keep them separate, I think discussion of values is inherent in the assessment process. This can be seen in two ways.

First is the bounding or scoping problem, that is, the assumptions which set the limits and scope of the attempted assessment. Porter *et al.* (1980) notes that bounding "is difficult to accomplish, deeply intertwined with other assessment tasks, and crucial to the effective conduct and completion of an assignment" (pp. 66-67). They report that in one analysis, half of the TAs studied were "severely impaired" (p. 67) by bounding problems. If bounds are set too early or too narrowly, the TA may be irrelevant. If set too late or too broadly, it loses focus (not to mention what it does to the time-table and budget). Porter *et al.* list six areas requiring bounding: time horizons; spatial extent; institutional involvements; technology and range of applications; impact sectors; and price options (pp. 67-69). All of them require making assumptions and judgements. Values are inherent in the process.

Even if the bounds are well defined, definitional problems remain. For example, a major impetus to introduce computers is to increase "productivity". Any TA of computers will have to look at their impact on productivity. Yet how is productivity to be defined? Definitions applicable to manufacturing exist, but do they apply to the office, let alone to the university? Furthermore, are the definitions we have limited by their relevance to an industrial economy? When it comes to productivity, "we don't even know how to measure it or even talk about it sensibly in terms of the information age, much less stimulate it effectively" (Cohen and Shannon, 1984: 45). In setting definitions, as with other bounds, judgements and assumptions, and hence values, are inherent in the process.

Additionally, the sponsors of a study usually have a say in setting boundaries. This makes the bounding problem a question of power. If the answers received depend upon the questions asked, who asks the questions? Who sets the agenda? Who defines terms? In other words, at its foundation assessment comes down to a question of *qui bono* (Whose good?) At the most simple level, this is seen in the acceptance or rejection of TAs by policy-makers. As Berg and Rich report: "One of the most significant factors found to affect utilization of TA studies was whether their potential users found them helpful or detrimental to the interests of their organizations" (Boroush *et al.*, 1980: 281). Such institutional self-interest can play a role from beginning to end in a study. The question of productivity, to continue the example, is part of the agenda of management. To even ask about productivity reveals a set of assumptions about the nature of work and the purpose of the organization, as well as the class perspective of those doing the asking. Equally important are those questions which are left off the agenda. Unasked questions are just as revealing of assumptions and perspectives. Once more, values are inherent in the process.

A second way in which values are inherent in the assessment process shows itself through the argument over methodology. Even since Descartes, the mechanical paradigm has looked to methodology as a means of escaping bias and guaranteeing certainty. A wide variety of methods have been developed for use in TA. From the beginning, a heated debate has raged between the advocates of quantitative and qualitative methodologies. Sherry Arnstein sums up the argument:

> In addition to being able to establish viable cause-and-effect relationships among the many variables involved, current quantification methods are not adequate for such unique tasks as (1) determining social acceptability and marketability of a new technology, (2) establishing, in advance, the dynamics of public attitudes towards future technological innovation, (3) anticipating changes in social values and perceptions 20-25 years hence, (4) tracing interactions among potential impacts of an innovation, and (5) distinguishing between facts and value based judgements. Having established that quantitative data alone are inadequate for these tasks, some of the practitioners were even more critical of

current tools and methods for qualitative analysis, since these lack credibility, particularly to those scientist-experts who reject data that cannot be empirically validated (Boroush *et al.*, 1980: 56-67).

These criticisms, although directed to TA methodologies, echo a growing debate within the social sciences (e.g. Bellah *et al.*, 1985; Lowrance, 1985, MacIntyre, 1985). The claims made by the traditions of the mechanical paradigm that their methodologies yield "objective" results with "predictive" power do not stand up to critical scrutiny. There are many arguments here, but nowhere are the issues clearer than in the problem of prediction.

Prediction, or forecasting, is an essential element of technology assessment, indeed, of all assessments. The process "requires the projection of the future state of a technology so that its impact can be assessed" (Porter *et al.*, 1980: 111). Unfortunately, "the record of social scientists as predictors is very bad indeed, insofar as the record can be pieced together" (MacIntyre, 1985: 89). For instance, Furnas' notable study (1936) on the future of science totally missed atomic bombs, computers and space flight. Over the past 15 years, no one has been able to accurately predict the gyrations in the price of oil, in and of itself only one component of the economy. Needless to say, economic forecasts are most noted for being wrong. More tragically, recent events have demonstrated that predictions of the nuclear power industry on reactor safety are equally invalid. The record of futurologists is little better than that of science fiction writers. Yet new, unforeseen situations and technologies could have a tremendous effect on the impact of a technology currently being assessed.

In part, this is a problem which is structurally built into the TA process. As the OECD reports:

> The major stumbling block appears to be the absence of a means of illuminating future trends in a manner relevant for formulation of feasible public policies. Here the difficulty lies in the fact that technology assessment is supposed to identify potential impact areas and evaluate their long-term consequences, whereas decision-making is usually sharply focused and short-term. This discrepancy seems to set political limits to the assessment function (1983: 13).

Science fiction may speculate on the future, but TA is supposed to be linked to policy formation. The kind of studies which may be the most insightful are not often funded, or if funded, not often implemented. Policy-makers want to know about the issues of the day.

But the essence of the prediction problem is deeper. In spite of well-developed quantitative and qualitative methods, Porter *et al.* are forced to admit that "methodological sophistication contributes little to the accuracy of forecasts" (1980: 112). Simple extrapolations or judgement calls are as accurate as the most complex models and simulations. They add: "Basic core assumptions, not derivable from methodology, are the major determinants of forecast accuracy. When the core assumptions are valid, the choice of method is either obvious or secondary. When they are wrong, methodology can make little difference" (p. 112). They point out one additional factor – "The time horizon is the most consistent correlate of accuracy" (p. 113). In other words, it is easier to guess what is likely to happen next year than 10 years hence. But this is a truism. The implication of what Porter *et al.* are saying (and which they apparently don't recognize themselves (since they go on to discuss methodology at great length) is that values rather than method is the key to "prediction". What counts are the paradigms the forecasters are working within. Why is this so? I think there are two reasons.

First is our poor record in prognosticating that which is totally new. The various methodologies for prediction rely upon extrapolations of present trends or simulation of the current system. As soon as something new enters the picture, these sort of projections will be thrown off. Even relatively minor changes in the dynamics of a social system can distort forecasts. This problem is inherent in predictive methodology. Either the forecast is based solely on current data and trends, and therefore cannot encompass anything new, or assumptions about changes are introduced into the model by the researchers. But if that is done, the whole exercise is only as good as those assumptions. What counts, then, is the adequacy of the forecaster's understanding of causality (that is, the paradigm of technological and social change) and her or his imaginative abilities. One creative insight may have more validity than all the models based on the *status quo*.

Secondly, as soon as recommendations are made, they become part of the information upon which people base their decisions. Whatever inferences and extrapolations are made, whatever trends discerned, are liable to change simply because people now know about them. The TA itself becomes a part of the future which it was trying to predict. Prediction requires a determinate future, but, as I think Giddens (1984) quite correctly maintains in this context, people reflexively create their own futures. Inevitably, TA engages in a process of self-fulfilling or self-defeating prophecies.

Is the question of prediction the wrong question? Is the real problem one of foretelling or of forthtelling? That is to say, is prediction really about decreeing what the future will be, or is it in reading the "signs of the times", the trends and tendencies, so that people can make purposeful and (reasonably) informed actions? If the latter, the burden of "prediction" shifts from the aracanities of methodology to the values of the content. What matters is not accuracy of indicators but responsibility of recommendations. In the assessment process, we must understand that we are not "predicting" the future but participating in creating it. What counts is our praxis.

Through both the bounding problem and the argument over methodology then, we can see that discussion of values is inherent in, and fundamental to, the assessment process. Without an adequate understanding of values, assessment lacks sufficient standards and criteria for evaluation. This is precisely the second problem which over-reliance on the mechanical paradigm of science has given TA: an inadequate conception of value.

Adherents of the mechanical paradigm assume that there is a clear distinction between facts and values and that when the researcher "begins to 'evaluate', causal analysis almost always ceases – to the prejudice of the scientific results" (Max Weber, 1949: 33). Only empirical facts are objective. When values are the object of study, they are defined as "social facts", to be treated like any other empirical data. The norm for the researcher is to remain "unbiased", "objective" and "non-judgemental". The emphasis of any study thus shifts to methodology, since only the most rigorous methods will be able to control bias and ensure value-neutrality.

Since most of those who do technology assessment operate within the mechanical paradigm, these assumptions create problems for the assessment process. They are caught between their need for practical evaluation and their commitment to "scientific objectivity". Even those who recognize the importance and inescapability of value commitments to assessment are trapped in this dilemma. For example, Porter *et al.* go further than most in recognizing that "there is no precisely value-neutral position from which any assessment can be conducted" (1980: 45). But this insight is simply grafted onto their commitment to "follow established scientific principles and procedures" (p. 46). The most they can do is call for "balance" and "recommend" a value-explicit approach (p. 45) in which "the assessors should try to spell out their assumptions and make clear their personal allegiances, so that the users of their study can judge the positions taken" (p. 45). Their understanding of values is fundamentally individualistic. Values are personal proclivities. They are seen as "choices" of the individual researcher which, like a hand of cards, are "held" and which can be "laid on the table". In their view, this value-explicit approach is as necessary to overcome bias as is methodological rigour.

While this approach is far more sophisticated than the crude positivism still evident in much contemporary social science, it still isn't satisfactory. I don't think their lack of success can be overcome by making a better "graft". The problem lies in their conception of values. Ernest Nagel claims it is almost naive:

> Although the recommendation that social scientists make fully explicit their value commitments is undoubtedly salutary, and can produce excellent fruit, it verges on being a counsel of perfection.... The difficulties generated for scientific inquiry by unconscious bias and tacit value orientations are rarely overcome by devout resolutions to eliminate bias. They are usually overcome, often only graudally, through the self-corrective mechanisms of science as a social enterprise (Lowrance, 1985: 55).

It is in praxis that bias is revealed, and overcome.

It is precisely in praxis that the weaknesses of their conceptions of values becomes apparent. One of the chief failings of TA, the OECD acknowledges, is that "relatively little attention has been paid to the fundamental point of technology assessment, i.e. a workable definition of the public interest in the name of which assessments are launched and carried out" (1983: 49). They lack a concept of the common good. They are thus caught in a contradiction. Without a workable definition of the common good, they have no standard of evaluation. But their notion of values blocks such a definition. Recognizing this, they rather lamely respond: "Perhaps the most one can hope for, given that no neutral or generally valid definition of the common good seems possible ex-post, is that some kind of sufficient consensus will subsequently be achieved during the assessment process" (49-50).

Their understanding of values has become the chief obstacle to overcoming the difficulties for which they introduced the discussion of values in the first place. Their language of values is inadequate. Robert Bellah argues:

> It should be clear by now that "values" . . . are in themselves no answer. "Values" turn out to be the incomprehensible, rationally indefensible thing that the individual chooses when he or she has thrown off the last vestige of external influence and reached pure, contentless freedom.
>
> The language of "values" as commonly used is self-contradictory precisely because it is not a language of value, or moral choice. It presumes the existence of an absolutely empty unencumbered and improvisional self. It obscures personal reality, social reality, and particularly the moral reality that links person and society (1985, pp. 79-80).

An individualistic understanding of values cannot go beyond self-interest, the summing of private goods. But no calculus has ever been able to discover the common good by adding up private benefits. Only by actively searching for the good of the whole society can assessment transcend individual, organizational, or communal, or class self-interest. As long as they remain committed to a paradigm which separates fact from value, subject from object, and thought from action, they will never be able to achieve integration. As long as they try to make assessments from within a framework of assumptions which sees people and events as isolated nomads interacting mechanically, their discussion of values will be unable to encompass the common good. As long as they define values as individualistic, even idiosyncratic, choices which may bias a study unless carefully explicated, values will never be more than a graft on their science. Values will never be integral to assessment.

Once we step outside the assumptions of the mechanical paradigm, however, we open up the possibility of escaping this contradiction. Then we can recognize that instead of individual specialists, each with a personal bag of "values", we are all members of communities engaged in praxis. We are part of ongoing traditions. Critical examination of these traditions opens our discourse to discussion of the virtues of the community. Such dialogue changes the definition of "values". Discussion of values becomes a search for the common good.

This dramatically changes the approach to assessment. Discussion of values is inherent in the assessment process, and no longer a graft added on as one more guarantee of rigour. Such a dialogue must be proactive. It must arise out of our praxis, out of the practical application of criteria and standards to make judgements about technology. Only if we do this will technology assessment live up to its potential. Only then can we escape the illusions of technological mysticism.

APPENDIX

N.B. Throughout this paper, I assume familiarity on the part of the readers with the current debates in the philosophy of science over paradigms. For those not familiar with this debate, I include the following summary:

A paradigm is a structure of meaning which Thomas S. Kuhn defines as "the entire constellation of beliefs, values, techniques, and so on, shared by the members of a given community" (1970: 175). It is the way in which a community of inquirers organizes meaning. "A paradigm is what the members of a scientific community, and they alone, share. Conversely, it is their possession of a common paradigm that constitutes a scientific community of a group of otherwise disparate men" (Kuhn, 1977: 294). This emphasis upon community is crucial. Paradigms are not a temporal abstractions, or even theory alone, but arise out of the social practice of researchers. In other words, paradigms are conversations. The topics of conversation change over time, as do the individuals who take part, but the conversation itself goes on, defining the community of participants. It is, in Richard Bernstein's words, "an historical phenomenon that is analogous to that of tradition" (1983: 77). At its broadest level then, a paradigm is a worldview or set of fundamental assumptions shared by an ongoing group.

Embedded within these traditions, or broad conversations, are smaller conversations among more clearly and sharply defined communities. As the conversation becomes more focused, it centres around fewer but more specific issues. At these levels we are dealing with subsets of the paradigm, what Lakatos calls "research programs" (in Bernstein, 1983: 64ff.), Kuhn calls a "disciplinary matrix" (1970: 182ff.), or what in the social sciences are more commonly called "schools" (e.g. the Frankfurt School, the Chicago School) or "theories" (e.g. functionalism, conflict theory). We have then, communities existing at many levels. If we could visualize a paradigmatic structure of meaning, it might look like Fig. 10.1 (in the social sciences; at least). There are considerable differences between natural and social sciences, not least of which is that the social sciences are characterized by a multiplicity of basic paradigms, and consequently a pronounced division into "schools" (Cf. Kuhn, 1977).

Several criteria define a disciplinary matrix. First and foremost, "such communities are characterized by the relative fullness of communication within the group and by the relative unanimity of the group's judgement on professional matters" (Kuhn, 1977: 296). In the social sciences, this unanimity is perhaps more "relative" than in the natural sciences, but in both "normal" work is characterized by a common agenda or research project, mutual understanding of key issues, and shared approaches and methods. Further, a disciplinary matrix is defined by shared values (Kuhn, 1970: 186). Not all members of a community of inquiry will act the same, not all will agree with each other on every point. But on central questions, and in particular in making judgements, common values are decisive.

So a disciplinary matrix is a focused conversation. Communication between disciplinary matrixes or paradigmatic subsets – and even more between paradigms – is more problematic. Bernstein notes that:

> Rival paradigm theories are logically *incompatible* (and, therefore, really in conflict with each other); incommensurable (and, therefore, they cannot always be measured against each other point-by-point); and *comparable* (capable of being compared with each other in multiple ways without requiring the assumption that there is or must always be a common, fixed grid by which we measure progress) (1983: 86).

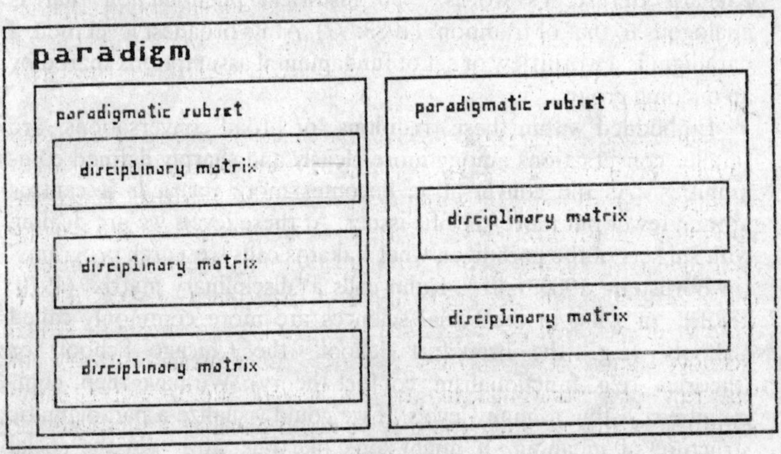

FIG 10.1: Paradigmatic structure of meaning

As one moves outward through a paradigmatic structure of meaning, the number (and often intensity) of shared beliefs, values, techniques, etc. declines. The extent to which theories are incompatible and incommensurable increases.

This last factor is what makes comparing paradigms so difficult. Verification rules are an assumption of the paradigm itself. What consitutes clinching evidence by one paradigm can be regarded as irrelevant by another. Their theories are not only imcompatible, but incommensurable. They lack a single standard by which they can be measured. Our task is, as the cliche goes, like comparing apples and oranges.

If paradigm choice is not to be simply arbitrary and unreflective, however, we have to criticize and evaluate. But it is precisely in criticizing and evaluating that I believe we can proceed. However different the paradigms may be, they are still comparable. There may not be a single standard of measure, but that does not mean there are no measures at all. Instead of looking for a set of "objective" verification rules, or succumbing to an irrational and arbitrary relativism, we have to test the arguments of each. To return to the cliche, apples and oranges can be compared, even if not by one set of standards. Richard Bernstein describes what we do when we compare paradigms:

> We can compare them in multiple ways. We can recognize losses and gains. We can even see how some of our standards for comparing them conflict with each other. We can recognize – especially in cases of incommensurability in science – that our arguments and counter-arguments in support of rival paradigm theories may not be conclusive. We can appreciate how much skill, art and imagination are required to do justice to what is distinctive about different ways of practising science and how "in some areas" scientists "see different things". In underscoring these features, we are not showing or suggesting that such comparison is irrational, but opening up the types and varieties of practical reason involved in making such rational comparisons (1983: 92-93).

The truth of any paradigm cannot be assumed, but neither can it be dismissed. All must be put to the test of argument. Between rival paradigms a great gulf may indeed be fixed. But it is never an unbridgable gulf. Comparability may become more difficult, but because paradigms are conversations, the possibility of dialogue and understanding remain. This may require subtle hermeneutics and a great deal of patience, but the result, as Bernstein concludes, "is not closure and being encapsulated in self-contained frameworks but the openness of experience, language and understanding" (1983: 108).

REFERENCES

Bell, Daniel (1979). The Social Framework of the Information Society, In Detouzos, Michael and Moses, Joel (eds.), *The Computer Age: A Twenty-Year View*, Cambridge, Mass.: MIT Press.

Bellah, Robert N., Masden, Richard, Sullivan, William M., Swidler, Ann and Tipton, Steven (1985). *Habits of the Heart*, Berkeley: University of California Press.

Bernstein, Richard (1983). *Beyond Objectivism and Relativism,* Philadelphia: University of Pennsylvania Press.

Boroush, Mark, Chen, Ken and Christakis, Alexander (1980). *Technology Assessment: Creative Futures,* New York: North Holland.

Cohen, Dian and Shannon, Kristan (1984). *The Next Canadian Economy*, Montreal: Eden Press.

Furnas, C.C. (1936). *The Next Hundred Years: The Unfinished Business of Science*, New York: Reynal & Hitchcock.

Giddens, Anthony (1979). *Central Problems in Social Theory,* Berkeley: University of California Press.

Giddens, Anthony (1984). *The Consititution of Society,* Berkeley: University of California Press.

Hart, Hornell (1957). Predicting Future Trends, In Allen, Francis R. *et al.*, (eds.), *Technology and Social Change,* New York: Appleton-Century-Crofts.

Kuhn, Thomas S. (1970). *The Structure of Scientific Revolutions* (2nd ed.), Chicago: University of Chicago Press.

Kuhn, Thomas S. (1977). *The Essential Tension,* Chicago: Univeristy of Chicago Press.

Lowrance, William W. (1985). *Modern Science and Human Values,* New York: Oxford University Press.

MacIntyre, Alasdair (1985). *After Virtue* (2nd ed.), London: Duckworth.

Mesthene, Emmanuel G. (1970). *Technological Change: Its Impact on Man and Society,* Cambridge, Mass.: Harvard University Press.

Ogburn, William F. (1957). How Technology Causes Social Change, In Allen, Francis R. *et al.*, (eds.), *Technology and Social Change,* New York: Appleton-Century-Crofts.

Organization for Economic Co-operation and Development (OECD) (1983). Assessing the Impacts of Technology on Society, Paris: OECD.

Pacey, Arnold (1983). *The Culture of Technology,* Cambridge, Mass.: MIT Press.

Porter, Alan L. *et al.* (1980). *A Guidebook for Technology Assessment and Impact Analysis,* New York: North-Holland.

Slack, Jennifer (1984). *Communiction Technologies and Society,* Norwood, N.J.: Ablex Publishing Co.

Toffler, Alvin (1970). *Future Shock,* New York: Random House.

Weber, Max (1949). *The Methodology of the Social Sciences* (Edward Shils and Henry Finch, trans. and eds.), New York: The Free Press.

11

SOCIAL IMPACT OF COMPUTER TECHNOLOGY: Some Research Questions in the Indian Context

BINOD C. AGRAWAL

My attempt in this paper is to raise research questions rather than provide answers. I am raising questions for discussion. I also intend to examine universal and culture-specific problems related to computer applications and utilisation in various aspects of higher education. The term 'higher education' includes bachelor's degree and above provided by colleges, universities and institutions deemed to be universities within India. By definition then, it includes all professional institutions, whether medical, management or music. In this respect, the universe of discussion comprises of 150 odd universities and over 5,000 colleges affiliated to these universities. At this juncture, it would be essential to differentiate between 'application' and 'utilisation' of computers in higher education. 'Application' denotes the possible areas where computers can assist or are thought to be helpful in administration, examination, finance, project management, research and teaching, while 'utilisation' refers to an evaluative dimension to find out the extent to which computers are being used to a variety of situations in the Indian higher education.

In a comparative study on the social impact of computers in higher education, these two aspects must be carefully analysed. The level of initial computer penetration should also be established in two different cultural contexts. The 'impact' is not conceived here as an unidirectional force whose thrust would accelerate the speed and bring about directional change. Rather it is thought to be a multilinear force leading to all pervasive changes that might occur over a period of time in the society as a whole.

In the Indian perspective, the debate which needs to be advanced relates to the influences of chip technology, both at the national and global levels. Recently, I have discussed this issue in connection with communication technology. Whether the term 'new', when talking of communication technologies, should be avoided as the technologies are not new; what has gone through remarkable transformations in its applications, resulting from the initiatives taken by the transnationals to convert the chip technology into consumer electronics for mass consumption (Agrawal and Kalyan, 1985:1).

In the same spirit, I would urge you to consider the use of the term 'high technology' in the present discussion. When we are talking of high technology in the present discussion, are we assuming that the technologies are vertically graded in a hierarchy in which computer technology enjoys the apex position? Is it qualitative and quantitative differences in the technological manipulative ability that differentiates 'high' from 'low' technology? Or is it the speed and accuracy of the computer that differentiates it from other technologies? I am raising this question to clarify our own minds on this issue.

The Contrasting Images in Indian Higher Education

Having taken a cultural perspective, a quick analysis of the salient features of the Indian society will help sharpen the research issues.

The multiple images that appear when we talk of the Indian society represent an historical continuity of several millenia. Here, several religious thoughts evolved creating contrasting ideologies and a continuous dialogue and quest for knowledge. At another level, it remained extremely stratified, which has been further accentuated as a result of industrialisation and ever growing urbanisation. "Education, *per se,* whether in the classical sense or in the contemporary context was and remains a victim of the very structure in which it flourished. From the ancient days and even today, it remains a preserve of the few. It would not be wrong to say that the Indian society is divided between the rulers having 'power' of education and the ruled without education. This bipartite division of Indian society seemed to have been tempered for the first time by the British education that seemingly allowed an open admission policy for brilliant students without any discrimination, a legacy that we continue to follow without any appreciable effect on the cultural ethos or psyche of the

Indian society (Agrawal and Kalyan, 1985:3). Professor J.P. Naik, an eminent educationist, aptly divided these two groups into the highly inegalitarian categories of abnormal human beings: (1) a small elite with big heads and small hands and legs which they could hardly use; and (2) a large majority of the workers who had very small heads but strong legs and hands. The system had also little scope for vertical mobility" (Naik, 1980:128).

It is in this kind of society where there is an existing educational gap between the few and the many that the role and utilisation of computer in bridging the gap must be studied. To my mind, the question raised for the present becomes a very important area of investigation both for us and our colleagues in other parts of the world. In the same context, one would like to raise the question as to whether computer learning, application and utilisation creates a new value system in bringing about a sense of equality among the fellow citizens, especially when the present educational system maintains a 'double standard' even within existing higher education. In a recent report, the University Grants Commission (UGC), while commenting on higher education in India, succinctly remarked: "A small minority of educational institutions at all levels is of good quality and compares favourably with those in developed countries. But access to them is selective and is mostly availed of by the top social groups, either because they can afford the costs involved or because they show merit, which, on the basis of the existing methods of selection, show a higher correlation with social status. But this core of good institutions where although there is open door access, the standards are poor. Consequently, it is in these institutions that the large majority of the people, including the weaker sections, receive their education. This duality leads to undesirable social segregation and to a perpetuation and strengthening of inequalitarian trends in our society" (quoted from Indira Gandhi National Open University Project Report, 1985: 8).

In the light of these observations, a moot question for investigation then would be, to what extent is computer in its various facets minimizing undesirable social segregation and breaking of the inequalitarian trends. An answer to this question would be vital for the educational planners and policy-makers. It will help to understand the extent to which computers would help the spread of higher education with distributive justice in India and elsewhere.

Computer and National Policy on Education – 1986

The National Policy on Education, 1986, considers higher education "at the apex of the educational parameter" and envisages the use of computers in several aspects of university education and management. "As computers have become important and ubiquitous tool, a minimal exposure to computers and a training in their use will form part of professional education" (National Policy on Education, 1986: 17). Further, it recognizes that modern communication technologies have the potential to bypass several stages and sequences in the process of development encountered in early decades" (National Policy on Education, 1986: 22). In view of these statements, it is clear that the new education policy not only recognizes but forcefully plans to utilise computers in higher education. The effort required at the moment is to investigate within the Indian educational environment the special areas of applications and utilisation. This would necessarily demand an evaluative study and the state of art regarding computers in higher education. At this point, the studies in other parts of the world, such as Canada, would be of immense help as they will provide another level of computerisation of higher education within their cultural context.

Any study related to social impact of computer technology within the Indian context must seriously raise the related question of training and retraining of the existing professional human power in educational institutions. This would enable the educational planners and technologists to decide the speed and technological configurations required in the future if computers have to be meaningfully integrated and demystified for the large majority of the users in the institutions of higher education. The key to computerisation in educational management lies in the "decentralisation and the creation of a spirit of autonomy" (National Policy on Education, 1986: 26). Such an investigation would be of immense value in the coming decade as the educational planners have drawn the 'Programme of Action' for the integration of computer education in professional and general education courses at the first degree level.

Initial Experiences from Computer Literacy in India

At the moment, there are not many studies that have been conducted in India related to computers in higher education, although a number of universities and institutions of higher learning have been using computers for a variety of purposes. Important among these relate to research and development activity. The second use has been in the preparation of result and other management activities. Some efforts to consolidate present state of the art in it has yielded very marginal results due to paucity of available studies. At present, a large scale evaluation has been made of a computer literacy project known as 'Computer Literacy and Studies in Schools" (CLASS).

The Department of Electronics and the Ministry of Education, Government of India, undertook a pilot project on Computer Literacy and Studies in School (CLASS) with a primary objective of 'demystifying' computers by developing a broad understanding and familiarity with computers. About 250 higher secondary schools and intermediate colleges were provided with BBC micro computers in the first phase. On the request of the Department of Electronics, ISRO undertook a comprehensive evaluation of this pilot project.

The aim of this evaluation was to analyse and understand various components of the project in its totality. Such an understanding was considered very important because the introduction of computers in the school system was considered to "... have a liberalising effect on the schools and will make teachers sensitive and capable of utilising computer for improving the effectiveness of instruction" (CLASS Report, 1984). The main aim of CLASS, as defined in various documents, is to 'demystify' and 'develop a degree of ease and familiarity with computers' (CLASS Report, 1984: 3).

In CLASS evaluation, an *inter* and *multi* disciplinary approach was adopted. It involved computer experts, educationists, social scientists, electronic engineers and management experts. Accordingly, the evaluation responsibility of CLASS Project was handled by a core group of multi-disciplinary experts. Two main studies involved a large scale survey and six in-depth holistic studies. Broadly, in each study, school selection and installation of computers, computer performance, ulitisation and cost and overall effects and computer learning were studied. For this purpose the academic year of 1985-86 was taken into consideration, although the CLASS project started in the academic year of 1984-85. The delay in evaluation was because computers could not be installed in time. While the research reports are still under consideration, some salient issues that have emerged should provide some insight to us.

Computer as an educational tool and computer as a service

facility within the educational system is not a questionable proposition. The students' enthusiasm to learn about computers and to use computers for learning make it clear that the higher secondary school boys and girls are excited about learning the computers. Are there differing patterns of computer learning behaviour between men and women needs to be studied. Given the cultural norm which demands that physically strenuous jobs should be done by men and delicate work by women, one would be interested in investigating whether the computer falls into the delicate or strenuous category of jobs. The same rule applies for job opportunities for computers, or would it reverse leading to sex discrimination in the recruitment and selection of computer students.

Demystification of computers seems to be much less of an issue as far as the students are concerned. It is the teachers and educationists who feel that the demystification of communication technologies is required. The question raised here is whether there is an inherent value linked with computer learning or whether it emanates a particular value system, or it remains a means like any other method of learning adopted so far, or the innovative nature of the computers and the job opportunity that it provides has something to do with the way demystification might be taking place.

The higher socio-economic background of the parents, education in English medium of the students, seemed to provide favourable conditions for computer learning. One would like to know to what extent these factors have effects in the use and application of computers in higher education. More than anything, human factors and management structures seem to be either stumbling or facilitating blocks in the appropriate utilisation of computers in higher education. It would be interesting to investigate the extent to which these factors have contributed in computer applications in the Indian educational environment.

Educational and Technological Dependency

The introduction of computers in education, including the recent experience with BBC computers in higher secondary schools, is dependent by and large upon imported technology. Along with the hardware which has its own economic and political implications, software is imported as in the case of CLASS project. In the past, not only was the technology imported but the inherent value system was also embraced. Whether computer technology is going the same way ought to be carefully studied. Our present educational system is reminiscent of the colonial era in terms of management, growth and development of academic disciplines. One would like to know whether the new models close to technology donors will appear after the introduction of computers in higher education. This is critical because it will not only create technological dependency, but may push the educational system from one model to another without necessarily being culturally compatible to our needs.

I have raised these questions to curl out some of the areas of common interest for future investigations.

REFERENCES

Agrawal, Binod C. and Kalyan, Raman N. (1985). Culture and Communication Technology in the Indian Higher Education: A Synergy or a Mismatch. Paper presented in the International Seminar on New Communication Technologies in Higher Education at Delhi.

Computer Literacy and Studies in Schools (CLASS) Evaluation: An Interim Report (1985). Ahmedabad: Development and Educational Communication Unit, Indian Space Research Organisation.

Indira Gandhi National Open University Project Report (1985). New Delhi: Educational Consultants India Ltd.

Naik, J.P. (1980). Educational and Vocational Preparation of Children. In profile of the Child of India, Politics and Programmes: 127-144. New Delhi: Ministry of Social Welfare, Government of India.

National Policy on Education (1986). New Delhi: Department of Education, Ministry of Human Resources Development, Government of India.

12

PROCESS RATIONALIZATION AND THE LIMITS TO SOCIAL ACTION

ASHIS GUPTA

Introduction

The introduction of computers into Indian higher education is clearly a necessary initiative. It should help improve organizational efficiency, bring classroom instruction on a par with what is available in other industrialized or industrializing nations, and lay the groundwork for sophisticated natural and social sciences research in the present and future. In attempting to rationalize existing processes of work, study, and research, it is likely that computers will impact upon numerous dimensions of the social fabric. This paper conceives the introduction of computers into Indian higher education as a significant action designed to bring about social change, and proposes to highlight what might be seen as certain inevitable limits to such social action.

The Dark Side of Technology

Technology has been described as "the systematic application of scientific or other organized knowledge to practical tasks" (Galbraith, 1979). If the introduction of computers in higher education is perceived as the introduction of technology into the various aspects of education, it is only because it will permit the division and subdivision of traditional educational and education-related tasks into their component parts. Not because of the mere presence of certain machines in classrooms and offices. While technology lends itself naturally to appropriation for task-oriented needs, it is also susceptible to exploitation for other needs.

The Soul of a New Machine is an exciting, 1982 Pulitzer Prize winning story of a group of brilliant engineers — arrogant, egotistical, temperamental — who built a state of the art computer for Data General Corporation in 1980. When the group got together in 1978, things couldn't have been more rocky and chaotic. What a way to design a computer! There was no grand design; just people reaching out in the dark, touching hands. So thinks one of the engineers. The author remarks: "They lived in a land of mists and mirrors. Mushroom management seemed to be practised at all levels in their team."

The story ends in April 1980 following Data General's formal introduction of the "Eagle" computer (rechristened Eclipse MV/8000). The day after the formal announcement, the regional sales manager in New York was addressing his sales personnel. "What motivates people?" he asked. He answered his own question, saying, "Ego and the money to buy things that they and their families want." The book ends with the author's final, ironic comment: "It was a different game now. Clearly, the machine no longer belonged to its makers."

Unbeknown to itself, *The Soul of a New Machine* becomes a powerful critique of Western economic systems which have played such a significant role in the development of information technologies. Engineering and other innovations may be prompted as much by a desire to improve the human condition as by the hope of securing stock options, but the dynamics of the system invariably introduce less egalitarian elements as time goes by. It is not inconceivable that the New York manager's sales philosophy will be responsible for Data General selling or leasing its machines to Third World or other customers long after the shadow of obsolescence has fallen on the Eagle.

Such paradoxes riddle the entire complex of information and commodity flows that reach out to the *world's collective of nations*. Indeed, one may find the marketing philosophies of U.S. multinationals perfectly compatible with their notions of profit maximization and accountability to shareholders. As Milton Friedman, an acknowledged champion of capitalism, has observed, "Few trends could so thoroughly undermine the very foundations of our free society as the acceptance by corporate officials of a social responsibility other than to make as much money for their stockholders as possible" (Friedman, 1982: 133). Unfortunately, the exchange of technologies between developed and developing nations cannot ideally take place within such an orientation. This was the orientation that has left such painful colonial scars on so many Third World nations. If developing societies are to receive technologies within the broad principles of capitalism, it would surely result in the perpetuation of an earlier exploitative system.

Economic Systems and Social Change

There is of course the choice facing developing nations that they enter into technological exchanges with non-capitalist countries. (Desai, 1984) Unfortunately, large number of industrializing countries have chosen developmental models which are all based on giving priority to the consumption pattern of the middle classes. Within this context, non-capitalist countries are no match for the capacity of their capitalist counterparts to transfer commodities and capital. It seems, therefore, that developing nations, in their quest for technological progress, are likely to be drawn into an unequal relationship with the major industrial nations of the world.

Developing nations are aware of the future implications of these present relationships. They are mindful of the historical evolution of capitalism which saw certain regions of Europe, then of North America, and even Asia, becoming core countries in a world economic system in which other areas made up the periphery. Since the 1960s, a majority of the countries in the periphery have therefore worked hard at developing a New International Economic Order. The fact that this new order is still to materialize reflects not only the opposition of the core countries but also the internal contradictions within the nations in the periphery.

The advent of the industrial age saw the gradual transformation of social structure that changed certain societies from agrarian to industrial ones. Thus began a period characterized by the accumulation of surplus which the dominant classes used primarily for consumption. Gradually, accumulated capital began to find its way into new investments. As a result, relations based on money became increasingly important. These relationships would eventually be reproduced outside the core — in the periphery — to serve the expansionist needs of the centre.

The nineteenth century saw a decline in the economic viability of the centre as it confronted the organization of the working class. There were now higher costs to be incurred not only for securing local sources of raw materials, but also for internal class alliances forged to meet the threat of organized labour. The centre responded to this setback by, first, centralizing, and then exporting capital at a hitherto unprecedented rate. This globalization of capital, which began around the time of the 1871 Commune of Paris, forced realignments between the monopolies of the core and the ruling classes of the periphery, and saw the hegemony over world trade pass from the hands of Great Britain to the U.S. While British hegemony rested largely on unilateral measures to enforce free trade, American hegemony relied on free enterprise. Thus, direct investment rather than trade became the cutting edge of U.S.A. core capital. U.S. power, and its allied institutions, became instruments for transforming the capitalist world in the U.S. image* — through the reconstruction of the world market, the transnational expansion of capital, and the spread of Taylorism and Fordism.[1]

Fordism represented a policy of relatively high wages aimed at transforming labour's attitudes towards, and motivations to, work by shifting them from the realm of production to that of consumption. Generally, it came to be associated with mechanical consumer durables. Taylorism, on the other hand, institutionalized the division and fragmentation of labour ostensibly for greater effectiveness on the assembly line. But this was nothing new. In 1776, when *The Wealth of Nations* was published, Adam Smith clearly saw division of labour as the main source of increased labour productivity. The system must incorporate the external and internal frontiers of human society to accomplish a uniform division of labour. We have thus seen, in stages, the internationalization of commodities in the nineteenth century, of capital in the late nineteenth to mid-twentieth century, and finally — since the end of World War II — the globalization of the labour market with the spread of multinationals and controlled immigration.

With 'increased productivity' sounding more and more like the battle-cry of developed nations harassed by sharpened competition

---

1. * When these institutions or instruments come face to face with contending, adversarial structures, the U.S.A. has no compunctions over abandoning the contest. Consider American withdrawal from the I.L.O. (albeit temporarily) and from UNESCO because of U.S. inability to influence policy and implementation in accordance with its ideological preferences. Or, consider the cry for protectionism against the same trade practices that have, for decades, contributed to the prosperity of the developed nations (with, of course, one qualification — the developed nations faced little or no competition and hence exercised virtual monopoly power).

from emerging economic centres such as Japan and West Germany. It is easy to see the possibilities inherent in technology. The development of technology, as well as its application, demand ongoing fragmentation of traditional tasks, increased specialization, increased routinization, and convenient transferability of functions between uniformly trained personnel unified by knowledge, for instance, of artificial languages (e.g. Fortran, Basic, Cobol) all of which unite labour across national borders even as it is subjugated within the boundaries of the periphery. It has therefore been suggested that the concrete forms of expansionism are determined by class struggles and not by an economic law that is the same throughout history. That is why the development of a capital at the world level is likely to remain fundamentally unequal. "Accumulation does not homogenize world society: it maintains and reproduces heterogeneity in new forms" (Amin, 1982: 168).

This is not to suggest that process rationalization ought to be resisted by Third World countries at all costs. A fundamental question which must remain outside the scope of this paper is whether a strategy of delinking is possible or whether it is outdated in the present state of the world's interdependence. Even a process of partial delinking, as was envisaged three decades ago with North-South negotiations, appears to be hopelessly bogged down (Sewell and Zartman, 1984). It is therefore possible that many countries in the periphery will choose an easy development strategy that impoverishes the weakest. It will be an attractive choice for ruling elites because it is likely to be supported from abroad by one country or another.

Constraining Class Structure

One may or may not accept the premise that the expansion of the capitalist system, or transfers of technology, somehow reflect a class struggle between capital and labour. It appears, however, that in the twentieth century such expansion or transfers rarely take place in the absence of structural conditions that promote competition on a global scale. The classic determinant of global competition is, of course, comparative advantage (Porter, 1980: 278), which occurs when a country presents significant advantages in factor costs or factor quality used in producing a product. Such countries become product sites from which exports flow to other parts of the world. But the products may simply be absorbed by enormous internal markets at prices which promise substantial profits to multinationals.

In the case of India, at least, the presence of a local capitalist class has intensified steadily since the beginning of this century. This development helped provide the minimal structural conditions (e.g. industrial enclaves such as Calcutta and Bombay) characterized by the commercialization of agriculture, the establishment of private property in land, and the recruitment of wage-labour for work in mines, plantations and industry.

The unfortunate outcome of the capitalist rationalisation of the world has been the growth of an increasingly large number of intermediaries in one field after another. There has been a proliferation of professionals, engineers, managers, technicians, and service personnel who are essential to the operation of the system and who live off a part of the surplus value that others create. The net effect in the case of India has been to further aggravate pre-existing class distinctions based on caste and kinship. This may be the reason why, despite significant build-up of industry since independence, the vast mass of the Indian people have experienced little or no improvement in their welfare, while the fruits of economic growth have been gathered essentially by a fortunate minority.

This fundamental barrier to the realization of social change may be ascribed as much to the lack of structural transformation to remove blockages in the way of development as to the lack of resolute will to abolish poverty and create a more equal society. As a result, from the past to the present, is its visibility" (Beteille, 1979: 33). Not only visible and rigid, but elaborate as well — a conclusion put forward by Gunnar Myrdal in his broad comparative and historical study of the economically backward societies of Asia and the economically advanced societies of the West. It is generally acknowledged that the continuing backwardness of Indian society has contributed much to the perpetuation of a system of social inequality.

Computers in Indian education imply the introduction of a very valuable resource into the social structure. A major constraint to social change will, however, be represented by institutionalized inequalities in access to and control over valued resources by individuals and groups in society. A further obstacle to social change in India is the "belief that each individual has a dignified, rightful place and function in the society, a belief which transcends the formal patterns of deference to caste, class and family hierarchies, but does not hold the promise of an egalitarian society."

Conclusion

While the introduction of high technology into higher education does not necessarily spell a dependence on foreign multinationals, it does strengthen the relationship between the industrialized cores and the industrializing peripheries. Indeed, the technological dependence of Third World countries could be a matter of serious concern in the years to come. The international pace of technological change is so vicious and so capital-intensive that securing the resources to keep pace with it might involve a reactionary and counter-productive revision of social priorities. The lessons from the technological obsolescence of certain industries, especially in the developed world, are all too clear for us to see. While it may be argued that a failure to keep up with technology might push a nation deeper into the pit of backwardness, the argument presupposes the ideal world to be created in the image of the developed nations of the West. The argument further discounts the possibility of "vaulting" into the technology of the future through planning and carefully addressing first the insistent priorities of the present.

The relation between groups and individuals having differential access to and control over valued resources has been, and will continue to be a source of social unrest. While one may speculate that this could lead to revolutionary change, the prospect seems unlikely in the case of India. But the foreign multinationals who generally represent the organizational fronts of technology do possess a capability for effecting change. With the advent of technology into Third World countries, there develops a sensitive network of autonomy and dependence involving individual, culturally distinct communities forming part of a nation-state and a giant multinational solidly entrenched within the nation-state as well as a larger transnational network. The multinational's autonomy and simultaneous linkage with the extra-territorial network allows it the power to introduce exogenous sources of change within national perimeters. The extreme secrecy surrounding a transnational's relationships with ruling elites in developed Western societies as well as those in developing countries often permits the virtually undetected introduction of some of the sources of change. It then becomes the task of historians to observe change and attempt to trace it back to probable causes. Since the task is of a speculative nature, it is seldom possible to secure unanimity over the nature of change or the factors that triggered it or even the time frame within which the process may be placed.

REFERENCES

Amin, Samir (1982). "Crisis, Nationalism, and Socialism" in Samir Amin, Giovanni Arrighi, et al. (eds.), *Dynamics of Global Crisis* (New York: Monthly Review Press, 1982), p. 168.

Beteille, Andre (1979). *The Backward Classes and the New Social Order*, New Delhi: Oxford University Press, p. 33.

Desai, Padma "The Soviet Union and the Third World: A Faltering Partnership" in *Power, Passions, and Purpose: Prospects for North-South Negotiations* Jagdish N. Bhagwati and John Gerrard Ruggie (Eds.), (Cambridge: The MIT Press, 1984). Some of the problems involving Soviet technology transfer have been discussed. As MNC's have shown greater willingness to part with a wide variety of generally more sophisticated and more efficient industrial technologies, the attractiveness of the Soviet Union as a supplier of technologies to developing countries has diminished.

Friedman, Milton (1962). *Capitalism and Freedom* (Chicago: The University of Chicago Press), p. 133.

Galbraith, John Kenneth (1979). *The New Industrial State* (Boston: Houghton Mifflin Company, 1979), p. 12.

Porter, Michael E. (1980). *Competitive Strategy*, New York: The Free Press, p. 278.

Sewill, John W. and Zartman, I. William (1984). "Global Negotiations: Path to the Future or Dead-End Street?" in *Power, Passions and Purpose*. Bhagwati and Ruggie (eds.).

13

MANAGEMENT IMPLICATIONS: Computers in Administration

L.R. SYMES

Introduction

If one were to ask if the issues and problems associated with the use of computing as a tool in the administration of a university are unique, the answer would, of course, be no. A student information system is in many ways similar to an airline reservation system, and of course a payroll system is a payroll system.

While the application of computer technology to aid in the administration of a university is not unique, universities have some built-in advantages that are not normally available to other organizations. Frequently, initial acquisition of computing equipment has been made for academic reasons, and because of the initial 'surplus' capacity, time is available to incubate administrative applications. Further, universities with Faculties of Administration or Departments of Computer Science have a ready pool of expertise that may be used to provide advice regarding administrative systems.

Gibson and Nolan wrote a paper (1974), which attempted to explain the problems associated with electronic data processing (EDP) management by looking at how data processing departments grow and how they fit into an organization's structure at various stages in that growth. The above authors noticed when they reviewed the Computer Department budgets of a number of organizations that, over time, the budgets formed an S-shaped curve. From this observation they postulated the thesis that, since there were three shifts in the slope of the curve, there were four distinct stages in the development of an EDP department:

– initialization
– expansion
– formalization
– maturity

Further, they contend that an organization must pass through each of the four stages. That is to say, that it is necessary to solve the problems associated with each stage if one is going to pass into the next stage, "without a crisis and if the growth of the resource is going to be managed to yield maximum benefit" (Gibson and Nolan, 1974) to the organization.

Four Stages of EDP Development

Let us look briefly at each of the four stages proposed by Gibson and Nolan, and describe the various characteristics of each stage:

Stage 1 – Initialization

When a computer is first introduced into an organization, its introduction is normally justified on the basis that it will save the organization money. Consequently, senior management spends little time considering the long-range impact of their decision to acquire computing on either the organization or its personnel. They normally assign responsibility for the managing of the facility to the department which originated the request for its installation. This assures that immediate costs and benefits can be identified, but does little else, for one can be assured that the chosen department will jealously protect its autonomy and control. As a result of this protection, the development of applications from other areas will be inhibited. Further, when the time finally arrives that the EDP function should be controlled by a separate unit, conflict usually will erupt; this conflict may lead to management turnover at worst, and to a lingering hostility at best.

A significant problem that is normally overlooked during Stage 1, or merely given lip service, is the effect that computerization will have on employees. This problem, while always present, can be fatal during Stage 1. The best policy is to provide all employees with the most up to date and accurate information possible. Undoubtedly, fear and rumours are bound to develop with respect to the loss of jobs and the changes that are going to take place because of the introduction of EDP. "Management can make no bigger mistake than to falsely reassure all concerned that the computer will not change their work or that it will mean no less work for everyone. Such comfort blankets lead to credibility gaps that are notoriously hard to close. . . . . Depending upon circumstances, management directions may best be communicated downward by an outsider, by a department head, or by the new EDP manager. In settings where employees are rarely informed of management planning, it may even be wise to explain to the echelons why they are being given the explanation; again, in settings where echelons have participated in planning a formal presentation may be less effective than an open group discussion." (Gibson and Nolan, 1974)

Stage 2 – Expansion

With the introduction of computing there is normally an accompanying excess in capacity which quickly triggers a significant growth in the applications attempted. Some user departments will be prudent and could justify their applications, but in a significant number of cases the user is simply attracted by the desire to climb onto the band wagon, thereby attempting to acquire the status which comes from being a user. The growth that ensues quickly requires new and more specialized staff who quickly join with those that are already in the EDP Department in acquiring what might best be described as a 'superman' attitude towards development. They are not driven by organizational objectives or needs, but rather by the technological challenge which the project presents. The EDP Department quickly develops a loosely controlled working environment, and the users tend towards what might be described as pie-in-the-sky applications. The result is over-optimism and over-confidence which quickly leads to overruns – in both cost and time to complete systems.

The dilemma for senior management is the need for control on the one hand, versus two competing needs. One is the need for experimentation to gain experience and the other is the need to motivate the group of specialists who might become disenchanted if the work environment is overly controlled.

During this stage, as the EDP Department grows, there is the need to select middle management personnel for EDP to provide a measure of control. Where possible, these middle management personnel should be obtained from within. This provides a career path for those capable of balancing organizational needs with professional and technical interests.

Stage 3 – Formalization

An organization has entered Stage 3 when the following two conditions occur:

1. EDP budgets are in a state of uncontrolled growth. This will induce senior management to ask the question: "can we afford to employ EDP?" The response to this question is normally the establishment of very formalized control procedures.
2. The need to change EDP direction towards projects aimed at improving operations, revenues, and the implementation of decision support systems.

In Stage 1, most projects were associated with a reduction of administrative expenses such as clerical personnel in the accounting or examination timetable functions. In Stage 2, projects were initiated which would reduce the cost of goods and services – for example, an inventory control system. However, at Stage 3, systems are starting to appear that affect the strategic decision-making process of the organization. Such systems are going to affect the ways in which managers do their jobs.

To manage the transition through Stage 3, three actions are recommended:

First, components of EDP are probably going to have to be repositioned within the organization. This will involve the centralization of some activities and the decentralization of others. Centralization will undoubtedly involve the majority of skilled professionals, so that they will be available to direct their efforts toward new corporate wide applications. Conversely, routine activities such as operation and maintenance of existing systems may remain, or become, decentralized.

Second, a very senior management person should normally be made responsible for directing EDP resources. This may be supplemented by an active high-level management subcommittee, because as stated earlier, one of the characteristics of Stage 3 is the need to develop systems which will impact management directly. As a result, there will frequently be a need for either an organizational change or the sharing or shifting of various corporate responsibilities. If the responsibility for these decisions is not assumed at a high level, one can be assured that the individual managers will not cooperate sufficiently to permit them to occur.

Third, there is a problem associated with the positioning of the systems analysts within the organization. As stated above, there is a need to centralize skilled personnel. This, along with the establishment of a steering committee and other centralization in general, will likely have the effect of creating barriers between the users and the EDP Department. The users will probably perceive that they are being left out and left behind. To overcome this problem, it is necessary that some analysts be placed in the user departments.

Stage 4 – Maturity

Stage 4 is characterized by stability. This applies to budgets, the level of activity, and the location of EDP within the organization.

The problem one faces at maturity is a continuing competition between two equally strong forces. One is the need to maintain the steady working environment and the other is the need to keep up to date with technology.

The pressure to maintain a steady working environment comes from both the user departments and the EDP department itself. The reason for this is simple – neither group wants to change.

The need for change, on the other hand, is much more complex. Two of the main reasons why change is required are:

1. There is always a need to capture technological improvements. This is usually necessitated by financial reasons. As usage increases so does the need to acquire additional resources. Frequently the necessary resources can be obtained without an increase in budgets, by simply changing the hardware configuration to capture the technological price performance advantages that have occurred.
2. Some user departments will require services not currently

provided for by existing installations. Further, the manager of EDP has a responsibility to the organization to make sure that his organization is able to respond to innovations – desired or otherwise. The manager is ultimately responsible for providing technical leadership.

Other Considerations

When the only systems that were available were batch systems, there was no doubt who the real user of a system was. The real user or owner of a system was the department which collected data from various sources, had this data put into machine readable form, fed it into the batch system, and dispersed the output to those that had need to use it.

The introduction of online interactive systems brought with it a degree of decentralization that was not possible with batch systems, and leads one to ask the question in this new environment, about who is the real user, or owner, of a system. For example, while the registrar's office is considered responsible for the student registration system, with an online interactive system, the personnel in the registrar's office are no longer the only direct users of the system; indeed, they may not even be the majority user.

Frequently, institutions have not fully recognized the operational significance of a change in systems and have left the responsibility for the selection of the new system to the current user department or unit. When this is done, it is not uncommon to find, after the new system is installed, that while it solved the old problems, it has created a number of new and possibly more severe problems, because sufficient consideration was not given to the new users.

When an organization is planning such a change, it is essential that steps be taken to ensure that all affected user groups are consulted during the planning stage, to ensure that the personnel that will actually use the system are fully aware of their role, and that their needs have been accounted for in the new system.

For example, if one is developing a new system for the library to aid them in providing service to the education graduate students, who should be consulted during the design of the system? All too often the analyst will assume that the system is being created for the library, and will stop investigating after having talked to the staff member in the library who has been assigned the task from that end, leaving out any discussion with the graduate students in education for whom the system is being created.

Initially, employee fear associated with the introduction of computerization was normally limited to concerns related to job security. With the degree of decentralization currently available and the spectrum of solutions which can involve the use of a stand alone system through to the use of the central mainframe, employee concerns are now two-dimensional. On one plane is the old fear of loss of job, and on another is the new concern of job skills.

A simple example of this combined effect can be seen when word processing is introduced. Word processing is introduced into an organization to improve efficiency, and therefore has an effect on individuals concerned about job security. However, today the major problem with many members of staff is not so much this, as is the question of the job skills required. For while the skills required to operate a word processor are similar to those required to operate a typewriter, the skills are much more complicated and are much more difficult to master. Therefore, if the task of training is not given sufficient attention, one may witness a significant reduction in morale and as a consequence the organization may not achieve the anticipated productivity improvements, and may also experience general labour unrest.

The *I am unique* syndrome first appeared with the second administrative application to be put on a computer. The problem has, in numerous cases, increased the costs of administrative applications unnecessarily, by forcing organizations to expend a great deal of their resources re-inventing the wheel. Support for this comes from two quarters – the user department which is requesting the system, and the computer department which is to supply the system. The computer centre staff is motivated to support the *I am unique* syndrome, because for them building a system from the bottom up is much more stimulating than the tasks associated with maintaining and modifying a prebuilt system.

The motives of the user department are more complex. The arguments they put forward are based upon a need to satisfy a number of requirements which can best be met with a custom system. When these requirements are investigated, one will usually find that they are not as strong, as first presented, if one is permitted to change the organizational structure and the mode of operation within the unit.

The dilemma is that the user department does not wish to undergo change, and the computing department is not interested in pointing this out, because the outcome does not satisfy their drive to be creative through building.

Digressing for a moment, the small business man who wishes to acquire a computing system to aid him in keeping track of inventory, accounts payable and accounts receivable, normally purchases or leases a complete solution. After having his needs determined, he obtains the required software packages, has them modified if needed, and purchases the necessary hardware on which to run these packages. Prior to installation, he has his staff take the necessary training classes. Seldom does one hear of a small business which has such a system custom built.

It is true that the payroll system requirements of a large university may differ from those of a small university. However, the functions performed are essentially the same, and software firms have recognized this and are attempting to satisfy the market.

As a result, a trend is developing whereby institutions are purchasing packages instead of having staff build the next system in-house. A package acquisition policy, if adopted, while solving some of the problems associated with the *I am unique* syndrome, has its own associated management problems. These are related primarily to the question of how maintenance and modifications are to be handled. Does one maintain the system in-house, or does one sign a maintenance agreement with the vendor? And, to what extent does one permit the system to be modified in-house, instead of relying on the vendor to supply requested changes?

These two questions are not unrelated nor are they new, for the arguments put forward are very similar to those associated with the *I am unique* syndrom. When considering how the maintenance and modifications of an applications package are to be effected, the following two questions should be asked – is an applications package different than an operating system, and what are the real reasons behind the argument to do them in-house? If major maintenance or modification work is performed in-house with either an applications package or an operating system, what happens when the next version is released by the vendor? Either local changes have to be installed in the new version before it can be put into service or the new version cannot be adopted and the institution is left to fend for itself from this point on. Both of these courses of action tend to be more costly than having the vendor provide the service under contract. However, when first considered this may not be obvious in face of the immediate costs of the contract, and the pressure exerted by your own technical staff, who, as with all inquisitive people, want to take things apart to see what makes them 'tick'. Further, if one investigated the reasons being put forward by the user department in support of a local modification policy, one would usually determine that they are based upon the myopic perspective of the user department, stemming from its built-in bias against change – change that may involve organizational structure, but more likely will involve only procedural reorganization of the way in which activities are performed.

In today's environment, the question of system integration must be considered when developing policies for administrative use of computing. While the ultimate goal may be a total solution, reality dictates that this be achieved by taking a number of distinct steps. Care must be taken to ensure that each of the steps builds on the past. For one must always remember that once the first step is taken the next step is constrained. This constraint may be compatible with existing systems, it may be a question of equipment capacity, or it may be staff expertise.

Finally, associated with the operation of any system is the requirement to plan and implement back-up procedures and contingency plans. Back-up procedures include details such as how and when files are to be backed up, and how operational personnel can cover for one another, and to what extent spare capacity must be purchased. Contingency plans include things such as operating procedures that can accommodate 'normal' problems and delays, up to what is to be done in the event of a major failure.

Conclusion

The problems associated with administrative computing bring to mind what Withington (1983) had to say about the three laws of thermodynamics:

> "First Law : You can't win.
> Second Law : You can't even break even.
> Third Law : Furthermore, you can't quit the game."

REFERENCES

Brown, P. (1985). Managing Software Development, *Datamation,* April 15, 1985.

Gibson, C.F. and Nolan, R.L. (1974). Managing the Four Stages of EDP Growth, C.F. Gibson and *Harvard Business Review*, January-February 1974.

Nolan, R.L. (1979). Managing the Crisis in Data Processing, *Harvard Business Review,* March-April 1979.

Withington, Frederic G. (1983). Winners and Losers in the Fifth Generation, *Datamation,* December 1983.

14

DEALING WITH DISTANCE: Educational Challenge

R. BRIEN MAGUIRE

Introduction

Distance education is the most exciting challenge today in educational technology. Several communications and computer technologies have developed to the point where the potential and even the mechanics of delivery of educational material at a distance is within our grasp. These technologies include the transmission of voice, video and computer data by satellite, fibre optics, sideband FM and cable systems. The technology to store educational material at central and remote sites provides more cost effective winchester and floppy disk media. Recent developments in laser optics storage of images and data in CD-ROM or video disc format permit fast, direct access retrieval of massive amounts of data. Additionally, there is now widespread use of microcomputers by educational institutes and individuals so that there is a relative abundance of the computer equipment needed to deliver the lesson and tie together the other technologies.

Thus, the technology is available and all of it has and is being used to a degree by institutions in Canada. However, problems abound. These problems were parodied by Ross Paul in 1982 in a humorous "musical revue" (Paul, n.d.: 306) which included the chorus:

"Yes . . . technology's the answer, it gives you good vibrations.
You never have to worry about humanistic relations.
Technology's the answer.
It's the latest thing today.
Technology's the answer when you're far away."

and another refrain:

> "There's no worry about discipline or students talking back.
> A little bit of computerese will absorb any flak. So if you're short of tutors and student record clerks Just put it all on Telidon and let the machines do all the work."

Interestingly, Paul mentions the videotex technology, Telidon (Bown *et al.*, 1979; O'Brian *et al.*, 1982) that was and is still Canada's chief claim to innovative software technology with application to distance education. The irony is in observing just how little impact Telidon has had outside government supported field trials since Paul's parody. In the remainder of the paper we will review technologies applicable to distance education, discuss a number of ongoing efforts in Canada and consider the problems affecting distance education.

Defining Distance Education

By its very nature the term "distance education" suggests long distances between the instructor and the student. In the Canadian context most educators would immediately envisage a situation where class or educational material is being delivered or distributed from a city setting to a sparsely populated remote area. However, it is important to consider distance education to imply alternative delivery systems. That is, we will define distance education to incorporate all forms of delivering educational material that go beyond the confines of the traditional classroom, chalk and blackboard. Thus, applications from innovative satellite projects to the much older technology of mailing printed correspondence school material fit this definition.

It is particularly important to start with a definition that includes the growing demand for delivery of training and skill upgrading materials to urban professionals, the unemployed and the second wage earner in the family. In this context, the distances involved may be only a few miles but the only alternative available to the student may be to commute for literally hours through crowded city traffic. We cannot simply equate the problems of distance education to a distance problem and limit research to technologies whose primary advantage is to overcome that distance.

Distance Education Activities in Canada

The University of Regina model for distance education is quite typical of the activities of a Canadian institute which places a value on distance education but which, still typically, has been unable to raise the major funding necessary to implement an elaborate and high profile project. There have been, however, a number of innovative distance education projects using satellite or computer communications technology. Live two way video transmission by satellite has been used in tests to deliver bilingual instruction between Regina and several French speaking communities in Saskatchewan and Quebec (Wilhelm and Raineey, 1978). Microcomputer technology was used to implement an early "electronic blackboard" system for management training programs in Inuit cooperatives in the high Arctic (Thomas and Maguire, 1980: 967). However, as is too often the case in such experimentation, the profile and merits of the specific research project may be sufficient to raise the funding for a trial but the long-term provision of operating cost monies to leave the project in place is another matter.

The Faculty of Extension coordinates the offering of evening and off-campus classes for the University. In cooperation with departments responsible for academic content, Extension offers a wide range of credit classes throughout the whole province, an area of some 651,900 square kilometres. The total population of Saskatchewan is only 1,039,249 so the communities in which these classes are offered are quite small. The majority of the classes are traditional in nature in that an instructor is usually chosen from the local community and instruction is delivered in a classroom setting. In response to demand for more advanced classes leading to a two-year certificate or a three or four year undergraduate degree, Extension now offers teleconferencing and one-way videoconferencing classes on a regular basis.

Saskatchewan has an excellent rural telephone system and an innovative fibre optics network (Scan Report, 1985) spanning most of the populated portion of the province. As a result, the best options for distance delivery within Saskatchewan are tied to the facilities of the government owned crown corporation, Sask Tel, which itself owns and operates most of the land based communication facilities within the province. When the number of students at each site is very low, from 5-10, or the sites wanting a class are widely distributed, teleconferencing is used. Alternatively, videoconferencing is possible with classes in the five largest cities nearest Regina: Swift Current, Moose Jaw, Yorkton, Weyburn and Estevan.

Evening classes with students on campus are simultaneously televised to off-campus sites in these five cities with teleconferencing used to allow the off-campus students to interact with the instructor and students in Regina. Sask Tel also has a videotex system (Bown O'Brian *et al.*, 1979; O'Brian *et al.*, 1982; Scan Report, 1985) called Agritex which is used by Computer Science classes to provide off-campus classes with access to the mainframe computers on campus. While the system was implemented originally to deliver weather and agricultural information to Saskatchewan farmers, it allows 1200 band full duplex communication from anywhere in the province to Regina for $4.00 per hour. Microcomputers are used off-campus for introductory level classes to avoid communication costs and because of their suitability to these classes where BASIC and Pascal are taught. However, with the 1200 band data transfer rates of Agritex and the reasonable cost compared to long distance phone rates ($30.00 per hour for 101-115 km), more advanced classes needing access to specialised systems, such as large databases on the central mainframes, can be given off-campus.

The use of these technologies, particularly the videoconferencing classes, has been evaluated by our Faculty of Education and found to be effective (Keston and Burgess, 1985). However, the distance education classes have a relatively low profile amongst faculty and departments. Extension must actively lobby individuals and departments to offer classes. Part of the problem is a natural inertia in that continuing to offer the usual classes in the standard format is all that is expected of a faculty member. The distance education classes are all given in the evenings or on weekends, unattractive times for most faculty. Moreover, it is difficult to persuade faculty to repeat the experience after having offered one class by television or teleconferencing. Simply put, it takes more work.

Financial constraints limit the availability of support staff. Instructional designers, graphics and media consultants and support staff that could help the instructor package teaching materials in a format best suited to television delivery, for example, are not available. Often faculty must also become technically proficient in areas such as the use of microcomputers that are not part of their area of expertise or interest. The first occasion or two where the instructor must determine why the modem at a remote site does not autodial or why last week's computer password no longer works is a novelty. However, the novelty wears off quickly and the instructor comes to realise that there is considerable additional effort in using these alternative delivery technologies. All of this occurs in addition to fundamental concerns the instructor may have about the effectiveness of his presentation using the technology. The competent teacher will wish to invest extra time learning how to use a blackboard in front of a television or how to communicate by phone without the benefit of being able to see the expression on a student's face, for example, that says "you just lost me". Thus, there is a cost in technology related overhead as well as in learning how to teach using the technology.

The academic must weigh an interest in distance education delivery and the cost of the extra time and effort required against other pressures, particularly the pressure to maintain a reasearch and publication record. Compounding this problem over the past several years in Canada has been the pressure of heavy enrolment increases in regular class offerings. The reaction with many individuals, departments and even some institutions is disinterest or resignation that the commitment is impossible with the other pressures of regular class offerings. The reaction is one of "how can you expect to do distance education when we don't have the resources to handle the students we have now?" These problems and pressures exist at the University of Regina and at any institution whose primary function is not distance education.

Thus, at the extreme end of the spectrum we have institutions which, for the reasons just mentioned, have minimal or no distance education programs in place. The University of Regina is in the middle of this spectrum. At the opposite extreme is the institution whose sole rationale for being is to provide distance education delivery. In Canada the best known such university is Athabasca University (Ruggles *et al.*, 1982; Shobe, n.d.: 195). Originally heavily influenced by the British Open University (Branier, 1980: 293; Ruggles *et al.*, 1982), Athabasca has evolved to fit the Canadian context of larger distances and sparser populations. Interestingly, Athabasca has also evolved as a primarily correspondence university. It offers relatively few courses based solely or extensively on high technology. However, it does serve as an excellent role model for the provision of support services for instructors.

There is actually less faculty at Athabasca compared to the number at a traditional university. The number of instructional designers and support staff expert in the packaging and presentation of material far exceed the number of faculty. The faculty member is a content expert on a team of six to ten people which packages a course as a product. Faculty may or may not have a chance to evaluate the result with a traditional classroom audience. The success or failure of a course is usually conveyed back to the institution through tutors working in the larger centres where students are enrolled. A problem with course and programme continuity is that many of the content experts are hired on a counsulting basis for a single course. Thus, by the time actual students are using a course package, the consultant may no longer be available to help rectify any problems. Moreover, as most of the course material is in printed form, this material must have a lengthy shelf life resulting in large print runs. Therefore, it may not be practical to attempt to do more than minor repairs. Similarly, problems such as availability of text books over several years must be considered. On occasion, Athabasca has had to purchase the remains of publisher inventory to avoid supply problems such as a book going out of print.

Research Problems in Distance Education

As distance education is only one facet of education, research topics could include all the myriad aspects of general education. However, two points are of paramount importance. With respect to current and emerging technologies such as CD-ROM (Sehr, 1986: 79) which are affecting distance education, projects and research have concentrated on a single technology or one technology's advantages over another. Articles abound on the advantages and disadvantages of computer-assisted instruction, use of audio cassettes, video cassettes, videodisc and now CD-ROM cartridges. More technically-oriented researchers may be legitimately interested in cost performance analysis, for example, of satellite versus fibre optics networks. Such research is often the result of an individual's or institute's ability to acquire a novel piece of technology or to find a novel way to utilise existing technology. The difficulty with the results and conclusions of this research is the lack of a cohesive scientific model in which to place the technology and objectively measure the effectiveness of distance education delivery based on the technology. The term "integrated package" has come into vogue in the microcomputer industry. We do not have the equivalent in distance education.

We cannot afford this approach. The obvious reason is the cost of the technology. Failure to follow a scientific path and failure to integrate our technologies results in research projects that never go beyond the trial stage. Even if the trial shows compelling evidence of the merit of a certain technology or approach, the lack of integration means that new results cannot be combined with existing approaches. University administrators and government education departments are understandably concerned about losing existing investments in the "old" technology. An even more compelling reason why we must integrate our technologies is that we simply do not have the human resources to jump from technology to technology. Given the problems of attracting faculty to alternate delivery systems, we cannot afford to make those involved repeat learning curves again and again as technologies change and improve.

Certainly, technologies will change as communications and computer developments obsolete today's technology with tomorrow's promise of greater speed, resolution, memory and performance. However, we must begin to design delivery systems so that in accommodating the aging of present-day technology, we do not cause a rapid aging or obsolescence of our educational materials. For example, audio cassettes are no different from voice synthesis units or separate sound tracks on videodiscs or digitized speech on CD-ROM. All can be used to provide background music, spoken instructional material and, excepting the voice synthesis unit, can also store or transmit digital data. The challenge is to build a research framework in which voice and sound can be evaluated as components of the delivery system. Simultaneously we need to design systems such that new technology enhances the old. We could take lessons from component stereo systems which support several sizes and speeds of records and have incorporated audio cassette and compact disc technology as they appeared. Telidon (Bown *et al.*, 1979; O'Brian *et al.*, 1982) attempted to separate the actual hardware limitations of the videotex terminal from the picture encoding scheme. We need to attempt the same separation of the technology from the substance of the educational material. For instance, at some point in a lesson, the student may have the option to review an explanation of the prerequisite material. It should not matter whether the explanation is played from audio cassette or scanned from videodisc.

The other challenge we face is the need to evaluate how to

measure the effectiveness of our research efforts. Having suggested that there is too much focus on individual components of our technology, I also suggest that there is insufficient focus in our evaluation procedures. As a result it is difficult to assess scientifically the impact of new approaches or new technology. For example, all too frequently the conclusions of an experiment in distance education will be that "comparisons between the results achieved by both groups showed that the off-campus students did as well as the on-campus students". Conceivably all this has shown is that students in a remote setting with no alternative access to a credit course or training program can survive almost any piece of technology we aim at them.

We need control groups, more objective and more finely tuned assessment procedures as well as longer term follow-up assessment. In particular, we need to be able to reproduce results through independent experiments, the fundamental characteristic of a scientific approach. We must control the variables and factors being introduced. At Regina, a recent videoconferencing class teaching Pascal for the first time via television also incorporated off-campus programming consultants and a video overlay system to present programming examples, both again for the first time. It is impossible to comment objectively about any one of these factors. Grade results for on and off-campus groups could be compared, but, having introduced so many factors, can we say that they all worked to the students' benefit? Did the video overlay system used to broadcast real-time program development to the television screens at the remote sites improve student performance? Was it instead a negative factor in performance because the Pascal used was vendor enhanced and different from the textbook version? Did the off-campus consultants improve performance? In order to do scientific research into the use of technology for distance education and be able to answer such questions objectively, we need to be much more careful about mixing technology changes with other simultaneous changes in the teaching support environment.

Thus, in conclusion, the challenges are to integrate our old and new technologies and to develop a scientific framework for research into distance education technology.

REFERENCES

Bown, H.G., O'Brien, C.D., *et al.* (1979). Picture description instructions for the

Telidon videotex system. *CRC Technical Note No. 699-E*, November, 1979.

Bramer, M. (1980). Using computers in distance education: the first ten years of the British Open University. *Computers and Education.* 1980, 4. pp. 293-301.

Keston, C. and Burgess, J.O. (1985). A system evaluation of the University of Regina television project. Technical Report of the Education Studies Group, University of Regina. June, 1985.

O'Brien, C.D., Bown, H.G., *et al.* (1982). Telidon Videotex presentation level protocal: Augmented picture description instructions. *CRC Technical Note No. 709-E.* February, 1982.

Paul, R.H. Distance Education — A Musical Revue. In Daniel, J.S., Stroud, M.A., and Thompson, J.R. (Eds.). *Learning at a Distance: A World Perspective.* ICCE (Athabasca University, Edmonton). pp. 306-307.

Ruggles, R.H., *et al.* (1982). *Learning at a Distance and the New Technology*. Educational Research Institute of British Columbia. 1982.

Scan Report: *The response of Saskatchewan residents to a proposal for creation of the Saskatchewan Communications Advanced Network.* March, 1985.

Sehr, B.K. (1986). *High noon for CD-ROM. DATAMATION.* November 1, 1986. pp. 79-88.

Shobe, C.R. Systems approaches in distance education. (n.d.) In Daniel, J.S., Stroud, M.A., and Thompson, J.R. (Eds.). *Learning at a Distance: A World Perspective.* ICCE (Athabasca University, Edmonton). pp. 195-198.

Thomas, D.R. and Maguire, R.B. (1980). Computers and education: a remote learning application. Information Processing 80. Proceedings of IFIP Congres 80. Tokyo-Melbourne, October, pp. 967-971.

Wilhelm, B. and Rainey, B. (1978). *Saskebec ou la teleconference demystifiee*. Hermes, Royal Society of Canada.

15

USE OF COMPUTERS IN THE HUMANITIES: Potential and Problems

BRUCE F. MacDONALD

Introduction

The "Humanitics" as we now know them – literary and language studies, philosophy in its many forms, history and, more recently, the study of religion as an expression of the culture of human beings – developed in the West during the Renaissance. Humanistic studies were an assertion of the importance of the human being in the world, a re-establishing of the human scale, the human perspective, in the crumbling medieval world view.

The Renaissance humanists looked to the Greek and Roman cultures for inspiration because these early writers and thinkers seemed to reflect the sort of interest in humanity which the Renaissance wished to emulate. From those beginnings, largely literary and philosophical in nature, the humanities broadened to include any question about human beings and their environment. Thus arose the natural sciences and the social sciences as a more specialized expression of the interest in human environment and society.

In the nineteenth and twentieth centuries, the interest in science and the environment, especially in the means to manipulate and control the environment, led away from a concern with humanity to the development of a machine culture in the nineteenth century and now to the electronic culture of the twentieth century. The machines of the nineteenth century and the philosophies which accompanied them, led to a time of dehumanization in factories and cities, to problems of pollution and environmental destruction.

Perhaps the question the humanist must ask is, what will the electronic age bring? Is there the possibility for reducing humanity to a further sub-human level, of increasing misery and alienation? Or can the new technology lead to a greater humanization of our environment?

It is with some ambivalence, then, that the humanist looks at the new technology. Perhaps it is merely the remnant of the old nineteenth century conflict between humanity and the machines it produces. On the other hand, I have noted in the comments of many of my colleagues around the world, a suspicion that the computer technology has the potential to reduce human endeavour, creativity and thought to the mechanical level. If the machines of the nineteenth century assisted in destroying the skills of the craftsman, of the skilled hand and eye, is it possible that an advanced computer technology might gradually erode the skills of the mind which it replaces?

The humanist must recognize that the computer is an important artefact of our technological age, and as such must be studied as an aspect of human creativity. But something in the very nature of what the computer does, at least suggests a threat. The computer mimics the human brain: the question for the humanist is, how far can that mimicing go and what effect will that capacity have on human society?

The humanities, as an academic discipline, attempt to study complex issues of human culture, history, language, philosophy, religion and literature. Conclusions in the humanities depend often on an associative logic which, at its highest points, depends on a sensitivity to a vast array of possible options.

The complex awareness which is necessary for the best achievement in humanistic studies cannot be reduced to the "machine logic" of a particular computer system.

Computer systems depend on a simple logic of on/off switches. The computer system, even in advanced computer languages, must decide either yes or no, on or off. This sort of technological limitation forces any subject which is processed through the computer to take the form of the either/or. There are no maybe's in the computer.

Much of what happens in the study which the humanist carries out is done through what I will call a "tentative logic". Tentative logic recognizes that nothing in human affairs is absolute and that a discipline or technology which imposes absolutes cannot hope to arrive at valid conclusions about human culture and life. Thus, the computer cannot handle the everyday mental processes which the humanists (and researchers in other disciplines) use every day, processes such as: tentative steps toward a solution; suspension of judgement until more information is at hand; the establishing of multiple possible relations; metaphorical levels of meaning; the assessment of emotional impact or reaction; the study of possible symbolic associations; the use of imagination and the gaining of wisdom.

Computers cannot handle uncertainty, the kind of paradoxes and unanswered questions which lead human beings to the urge for completion and, through research and thought, to the growth of human understanding and maturity. In short, computers cannot deal with the emotions and insights and struggle for growth and creativity and beauty and inventiveness which make up the subject-matter of the humanities.

I have asked advanced classes in literature if they would like to experiment with the computer in the limited amount of teaching time which is available.

There was some interest, but so far the response has been largely negative, even though these same students use computers for word processing and other tasks. Their fear is that the introduction of computers into the classroom will so limit the range of possible approaches to a work of literature, and will place such constraints on our human, emotional, intellectual, sympathetic response, that it will be extremely counter-productive and waste the time they have available for learning.

This is a problem also in the social and natural sciences.

In trying to tailor our evidence so it can be processed by the computer, do we merely pre-determine that our results will be the image of the world as the computer can see it? To what extent do the results of computer analysis distort our vision of human capabilities? At least in the military we can see the results of seeing other human beings as blips on a video screen.

There are some very important questions we need to ask about a technology which the world seems over anxious to adopt in an uncritical fashion.

Does all this mean, then, that computers have no place in the humanities? Not at all. It merely means that computers cannot be expected to do the work of a sensitive human being. Let us turn for a minute to what computers can be expected to do in the humanities.

The scholar in the humanities does not spend all of his or her time trying to understand the products of human culture. Much time is expended in the mechanics of research, communication and teaching. It is in these areas that the computer promises to be of most assistance.

Data Storage, Sorting and Retrieval

One area where the computer excels is in data storage, sorting of information and retrieval of desired information. Since much of the work which is done in the humanities depends on the reliability and the availability of information, the computer can be extremely valuable in this area.

Libraries are perhaps the best centralized facilities for data storage and retrieval. Catalogues, lists of publications, bibliographies, lists of other resources can be computerized. Of course, all disciplines can benefit here. *As long as the computers are functioning properly* this storage of basic reference material on computer is useful.

Centralized data bases, to which all regional or national libraries contribute, make it possible for the researcher to gain ready access to information concerning collections of materials in every library in the contributing region.

If the databases are centralized and access is easy to all relevant data, then they can save the researcher many hours and days of searching. There is a very real problem, however, as databases proliferate without a standard format to make access easy.

There is the increasing problem of the specialist librarian having to bridge the gap between the complex technology now in use and the researcher who wants to spend minimal time learning to operate a computer system and maximum time working with the documents and information. The costs of many computer searches of databases are very high, as well, and cost is one factor which will prevent wide use.

Research aids can be made more efficient in some ways by the computer. Concordances of literary works or manuscripts can easily be compiled using computers, although they have certain limitations unless manual editing is also done. Interactive concordances are also now being made available, by which it is possible to have the computer search out the occurrences of a particular word or phrase and then call up on the screen the context in which that word appears, by sentence or paragraph or page.

Encyclopaedias are also being made available in the same way. Laser disc technology makes it possible to store, on a small disc, many volumes of material which can be searched at high speed. All occurances of a particular topic or name in what would be a 20 volume encyclopaedia can be identified in a matter of seconds and selections can be made as to which ones to examine in greater depth.

One laser disc can hold many thousands of pages of text and can be searched easily. They do not have the problems of magnetic discs, from which data can be easily lost, and they are becoming quite economical. It should be possible for a library to save considerable money, since even now an encyclopaedia on disc along with a reader, can be purchased for less than the cost of the printed version of the encyclopaedia. As more reference works become available on laser discs, the cost beneift will become more attractive.

The Oxford English Dictionary in currently re-editing their volumes with the aim of having a new edition on laser disc for economical and rapid access. Other major reference tools will swiftly follow. With costs of conventional publishing rising, this technology offers affordable reference systems for institutions faced with budget limits.

Another research development which depends on data sorting but which so far has had only limited success, is computer textual analysis. Any aspect of a literary or historical text which can be quantified can be analysed by computer. Thus, the number of occurances of particular words or parts of speech, the repetition of grammatical structures, the relative frequency of adjectives or adverbs or verbs and nouns can be identified by computer and conclusions extrapolated from the data.

Publishing and Communication

Scholars must communicate with each other. Traditionally this communication has taken the form of conferences, journals, books. Increasingly, computer technology has affected scholarly communication.

The word processing capabilities of the computer are at the heart of these new developments. Word processors can be used for composition, revision, printing and reprinting, communication over the telephone lines and communication with host computers.

The advantage of the word processor in scholarly communication is that text produced on a word processor can be handled in a number of ways without retyping. In Canada and the U.S., some government funding agencies require, as a pre-condition of grants, that journals or small publishers invest in "desk-top publising" technology – special computer typesetting programs and laser printers – to cut costs.

Some established publishers require that manuscripts which are submitted to them be submitted on computer discs to save cost on typesetting.

Journals need not be printed at all. Some journals, especially in the area of computer science and natural science, are distributed in whole or in part on computer disc. Some are stored in a central computer facility and subscribers dial in through their computers and down load from the host computer onto their own discs.

There is even room with some experimental journals for subscribers to make comments and through a system similar to electronic mail, to carry on debates over the wires.

An advantage of the electronic journal is that information and debate in a particular field need not wait for the long process of conventional publishing to get to the reader. Reaction and debate from diverse centres can be carried on on a day-to-day basis as well.

Problems arise with electronic journals, especially in the humanities where comparatively few researchers have computers or the technical knowledge to run them. Audiences are therefore limited. Costs of equipment and phone service, especially at a distance, are high. Questions of copyright and of academic recognition need to be worked out. Many researchers in the humanities are not yet willing to invest the time in learning the computer systems, time they could use in research more directly related to their disciplines.

It is perhaps not as essential for the humanities researcher, as it is for the scientist, to be always up to date on the latest discoveries. Humanists tend to take the long view.

Teaching

Most teaching in the humanities needs the human interaction, discussion, group exploration which only a teacher can provide. However, there are a number of areas where computer technology may be of potential value.

Many repetitive teaching tasks can be handled by a computer.

Some aspects of language teaching, for instance, require repetitive drills. Thus orthography, grammar, vocabulary and even sounds of the language can be taught through computer assisted instruction. The computer does not replace the teacher, but certain things that traditionally happen in language labs can be assisted by the computer.

Writing and composition can be improved through a number of interactive programs currently on the market. These traditionally have diagnostic tests and then exercises in those aspects of grammar or usage which the student needs to practice.

Logical concepts can also be taught through computers. Again, this involves the repetition of patterns of argument or logical concepts.

In early childhood language education and in literacy education for adults, computers have proved to hold a fascination for learners and thus have helped to motivate the learning process. Computer games designed to motivate learning are also popular among educators at the lower levels of the school system. Research on the use of the computer to teach humanities subjects at the universities, where levels of knowledge sophistication are much higher, has not been so widely developed nor has there been time for valid, long-term conclusions.

In the teaching field, computers and communications technologies seem to have found their greatest level of effectiveness in distance education, whereby the conventional classroom is extended over space or time to include a much wider student population.

Questions

The uses of the computer for the humanities can thus be summarized briefly. But there are some larger issues which concern me as a scholar in the humanities. These need to be addressed.

I have mentioned that the computer mimics the human brain. To what degree and in what sense?

The brain is divided into two halves and recent research has shown that those halves have different functions. The left brain seems to be predominantly involved in logical, linear thinking. It does not discriminate between elements of information. The right brain is involved in seeing patterns, in evaluation of information in the light of paradigms and learned systems of value. The left brain remembers language while the right brain remembers the music that goes with the words.

The computer mimics some aspects of the left brain function in humans, specifically the logical, linear thinking, the sense of the step by step process of cause and effect, the moment by moment of time. But neither the left brain nor the computer see the whole picture. For balanced operation, the brain functions with both halves, but the computer does not have another half.

Left hemisphere function has characterized much of our thinking about computer technology. So, people functioning with the left brain alone can nonchalantly continue to develop computerized guided military systems and, although educated to a high degree of sophistication, they never have to ask about the effect of those armaments on the people, cultures, civilizations who will be their targets.

The development of computer technology represents a refinement of the technological systems of a left brain culture, and their success is to a large extent a statement of the way left brain thinking has dominated our world economy.

Pure, valueless technology is the ultimate expression of the triumph of the non-human or the severely divided human consciousness. Our technology operates literally with only half a brain. The humanities attempt to present the balanced picture of human development. The humanities, then, even in adopting the technology, must assert that the computer is merely a tool, a refinement of one aspect of human functioning.

For years I have used a pen to write. Then I learned to use a typewriter for finished production, for neatness – that is an advance in technology. Now I compose with my familiar pen (it seems to give me greater access to right brain awareness) and then type and revise on a word processor. That is another advance in technology.

If the electricity fails, I always have my pen. That may be the next advance in technology.

This is just an illustration in perspective. The computer is a tool, a helper, a technological advance which helps to process information. It is useful and helps to contribute to a goal of expressing the results of research and thought.

Computers can process information, store, sort, catagorize, retrieve, transmit over distances. The vast amounts of information which we researchers produce can now be ama'ssed by computers into ever greater patterns and configurations.

This capability can be useful. But I suspect that researchers in India are the same as in Canada: we are faced with such a mound of information already that the prospect of the computer dumping a mountain at our door brings its moments of pause.

Do we need all this information? To what end? What has it added to our understanding of ourselves?

Over the past few years, computer theorists have assumed that "information" is somehow equivalent to "knowledge". We have even been dubbed an "Information Society". But again, information processing is one of those lineal, non-critical faculties of the left hemisphere of the brain.

The computer and the left brain do not distinguish quality or value; they cannot see the whole picture but only small bits of the picture (pun intended). The computer sees in "bits," one after the other in a series, never the total awareness.

Again, the humanist must assert the limits of this sort of technology. It is useful, but if accepted uncritically by governments or educational institutions as the replacement for human awareness – that is, integrated awareness of information and values – then we are headed for a time of decline in human and cultural values such as inflicts the end of most civilizations.

A report of the Association of Research Libraries in the U.S. and Canada presents us with a computer utopia:

> "A scholar sitting at a personal, multifunction workstation can easily manipulate large blocks of data or text; can store, test, and rapidly revise it through word processing systems; can have online access to bibliographic and informational databases; and can communicate with scholars on a worldwide basis." (from *The Changing System of Scholarly Communication*, no date, no place of pub.)

I find myself deeply at odds with this picture which is presented in context as a panacea for many of our academic ills. Like all utopias, I suspect it has the seeds of its own destruction within it.

What drew me to the humanities – an interest in the great literatures of the world, the thought and exploration of alternative ways of seeing the total human experience, the struggle of humanity with itself in its attempts to progress to greater understanding and awareness – all this is at odds with the vast collections of information and uncritical facts which we are accumulating like some great weight upon our backs.

What about time to think, to discuss person to person, to indulge in that creative rumination as we walk from one building to another? Perhaps because we in North America do not have the great ruins of civilizations of centuries past lying around us every day, we do not have the sense of the transitoriness of any phase of civilization or technology.

The computer will be with us until something more helpful comes along. We will find ways to use it, perhaps for our benefit. When the computer and the humanities meet, perhaps out of that meeting can come a sense of historic perspective, a feeling of the human scale for which the Renaissance humanists fought those centuries ago.

16

IMPACT OF COMPUTERIZATION ON WORK DESIGN:
Perspective on an Indian Experience

VINAYSHIL GAUTAM and R. THAIGRAJAN

Introduction

The popular belief that the computer revolution in management is not far off is fast becoming true. Compared to 10-15 computers worth about $30 million in 1955 all over the world, the number in 1978 rose to 60,000 computers worth $18 billion and the latest data put the number of computers to more than a million (CIER, 1966). The anticipated benefits of computer-base management system have been realised by the developing countries and, as such, their policies are fast moving towards greater utilisation and application of computers. In India, for example, greater emphasis has been now placed on computer education right from the school level and more and more institutions, including public and service sectors, are utilising it in their day-to-day functioning. However, these numbers are not as large as in industrialised countries.

An attempt has been made in this paper to examine the impact of computer-base management system on the members of the organisation and the work itself. More precisely, our focus is on: Are organisation structures becoming more and more centralized as a result of computers? Are these organisational changes a necessary result of computer technology or are other factors more important? How has the nature of managerial work changed? And how will higher levels of management be affected?

We may begin our discussion by briefly summarising the benefits of computers in, say, a manufacturing unit. The list will include:

reductions in cycle time from receipt of the customer order to shipment of original equipment and spare parts; reductions in inventory; more efficient use of manpower and machinery; reduced costs through elimination of indirect manufacturing expense jobs; and more timely, accurate schedules and management measurement reports (Myers, 1967). At a broader level, the benefits could be as stated by Christopher Evans: "Cheap person to person communication . . . favours the kind of open society and has just the opposite effect on autocracies – both right and left wings – who like to make sure that all information is handled firmly downwards" (Evans, 1979).

Despite these possible gains, we must realise that any form of technology should be understood primarily with the interaction of men and machines. The lack of knowledge and its consequences have been reported by various scholars (Volleborgh, 1981). One should be careful to avoid the alienation and frustrations of the kind which have been described long ago by such visionary minds as Kalka (Rathenau, 1982).

As such, one must examine the impact of computers on the work system and various categories of employees. For the industralised countries, some studies of this kind were conducted by Anderson, Rathenau, and Whisler (Myers, 1967). What we learn from these studies is that problems of implementation of computer technology is primarily a problem of the administration of change. For this reason, one should examine more closely the 'human' aspects of the change process, rather than with the technical aspects of the programmes themselves. We must acknowledge that while writing about the progress in the developing world, the limited coverage by scholars often restricts to draw any meaningful conclusions.

Centralisation of Organisation Structures

Wisler's (Myers, 1967) study on impact of information technology on organisational control has shown that computer-base information system often leads to centralised control in organisation. Functional areas such as accounting, reproduction and supply management, are also subjected to centralisation. Klahr and Leavitt (Myers, 1967) developed an analogy between computer programmes and organisations' structures: closed-routine programmes and organisations will move towards centralisation whereas open-routine or executive programmes and organisation will tend to be decentralised. Similarly

Delehanty, (Myers, 1967) while studying the life-insurance companies, found operational centralisation as a result of computers.

On the other hand, work of Deardens (Myers, 1967) indicated strong doubts and mentioned that it was the lack of time by top management to make detailed decisions, rather than the lack of information, which was the real reason for decentralisation.

It is thus difficult to say whether computers are making the system more centralised. Perhaps at various stages of organisational life, some amount of centralisation or decentralisation will be there irrespective of the change that is occurring in the information availability.

The Changing Nature of Managerial Work

Various terms are used to describe different types of managerial jobs – logistic, operations and structured, repetitive, routine, etc. Managers dealing with purchase, production planning and control, etc. perhaps will have fewer people reporting to them for the same volume of activity and they will be freed of this responsibility to devote more of their time to other problems. This also raises a serious issue – is it that the middle management group has shrunk in size as a result of computerisation? Delehanty (Myers, 1967) pointed out that possibly at a later stage of automation the total middle level group may shrink.

Forester (Myers, 1967) put the case for managers versus computers even more strongly. As computers are supposed to take over routine work from managers at all levels, there remain unstructured jobs that were not getting done before because these managers were too busy.

Let us assume a partial reorganisation of an engineering factory in which machine shops and assembly lines have been automated. The consequence will be a change of tasks along with the loss of certain jobs. Work preparation, production itself, and sales will be closer to each other. A new kind of broader specialist may be in demand.

Thus, the impact of computerisation could be seen as resulting in change of job and change in the structure or control system of the organisation. In Germany, attempts were made to estimate the number of jobs which change through the impact of information technology. It was found that about 50 per cent of the jobs will have changed character within about 15 years (Myers, 1967).

Yet another change could be shift from subordinate to supraordinate goals. Rewards will not be on the basis of their 'independent' accomplishments of the subordinate, specific goals in their own section, subsection or unit, but also include assistance in the attainment of the supraordinate goals of the total organisation. The possibility of losing control may cause (1) a great deal of massive resistance on the part of managers, particularly at the unit and subunit level, and (2) the demand that the programmes, at the interface between different sections or sub-sections come under manual control of the individual manager.

Effect on Higher Levels of Management

Many of the foregoing comments apply also at the higher levels of management where tasks are likely to be more unstructured and more 'amorphous'. The ill-defined, novel tasks on which top levels of organisations usually work generate flexible, open, non-hierarchical structures corresponding to participative management. Prediction is that the evolutionary application of more elaborate programmes will trigger 'a new wave of interactions and interchanges between organisations and computer programmes'.

Man-machine interaction systems, using real-time and time sharing computer technology may be particularly applicable at higher management levels. Carroll (Myers, 1967) pointed out that these systems can be flexible, providing data at the moment of decisions and offering capability to answer 'what if' questions about price policies, markets, product mixes, etc.

Robert H. Guest's (Myers, 1967) experience of General Motors' plant in using computers to reduce breakdowns indicated that as a consequence, the top managers had more time to work with their peers and subordinates on their problems. The perspective of the manager had been extended out in time.

What is Survey of India?

Historical Background

Survey of India (SOI) was established in 1767 to assist the then East India Company in conducting topographical surveys of their landholdings in and around Calcutta. Later, as the influence of the company grew in India, similar survey departments were established in Bombay and Madras presidencies.

One of the notable achievements of the department during the initial years of SOI was the Great Trigonometrical Survey of India commenced in 1802, with the active participation of persons like Sir George Everest (after whom Mount Everest was named).

The work of SOI increased manifold soon after India obtained Independence in 1947. The SOI has had to survey and map not only the various areas within the borders of the country, but also the inaccessible borders as well as off-shore islands such as Andaman and Nicobar.

The SOI has approximately 18,000 employees on its strength. While some of the employees have been taken from the Indian Army on deputation, some others are recruited directly from the civilian market.

Organisational Structure

The SOI, as shown in Fig. 16.1, is organised into nine regional circles and six specialised directorates/offices under the overall control of the Surveyor General of India (SGI), who has his headquarters at Dehradun.

The regional circles are the ones which accomplish the main tasks of surveying and mapping. Thus, the Directors of Regional circles report directly to the SGI in the present scheme of things.

Specialised Directorates or Offices, on the other hand, have been established with the main purpose of providing research and development, training, map production, satellite imagery studies and so on. The work of the Specialised Directorates, over the years, is being increasingly accepted by regional circles as an important component of SOI. Further, jobs such as printing or training are found to be acceptable to regional circles as centralised functions.

Output of SOI

The output of SOI is mainly maps in various scales and detail. Maps for use by airlines, defence forces, tourists, revenue authorities and so on differ in size and the extent of detail so reflected. The present output is considered to be woefully inadequate, considering the demand for maps on the one hand and level of accuracy on the other.

SGI

Regional Circles
- North Western
- Northern
- Eastern
- North Eastern
- Western
- Central
- South Central
- South Eastern
- Southern

Specialised Directorates/Offices
- SG's Office
- Map Publication
- Geodetic & Research
- Survey (Air)
- Survey Training Institute
- Research and Development

FIG. 16.1: Organisational Structure of SOI

Present Status of Computerisation and Their Impact on SOI

Computers of various degrees of power have been introduced in different regional circles and specialised directorates of SOI in the recent past. The computers that have been installed in-house are mostly mini and micro computers. On the other hand, specialised directorates such as Geodesy and Research Branch (located at Dehradun) use large computers for making large-scale mathematical calculations.

Impact of Computers on SOI

The impact of computers can be considered at two levels. These are:

(a) at the regional circle levels, and
(b) at the specialised directorate level.

At the Regional Circle Level

The work-load at the regional circle level is mainly confined to:

(1) field survey work, and
(2) office work for mapping.

While the 'field survey work' has not been affected by use of computers, it is the 'mapping work' at the office that has undergone some change.

Some Effects of Computerisation

Some of the effects of computerisation at the regional circle level are as follows:

(a) creation of a central service;
(b) importance accorded to a few; and
(c) work-load not shared by all.

Creation of a Central Pool

Before the advent of computers, a person who was good at doing calculations in a speedy manner using desk calculators and slide rules was considered important. But with the heralding of computers, a new breed of 'Bright Boys' have been accorded importance. These 'Bright Boys' have been given direct access to the top management which was not existent earlier (Figs. 16.2 and 16.3).

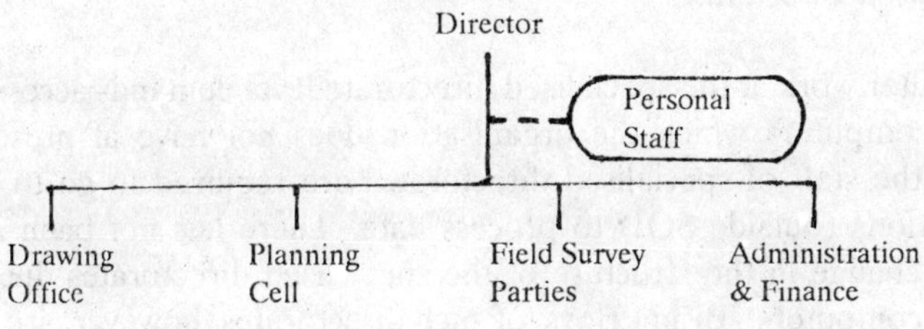

FIG. 16.2: Regional Circle Before Computerisation

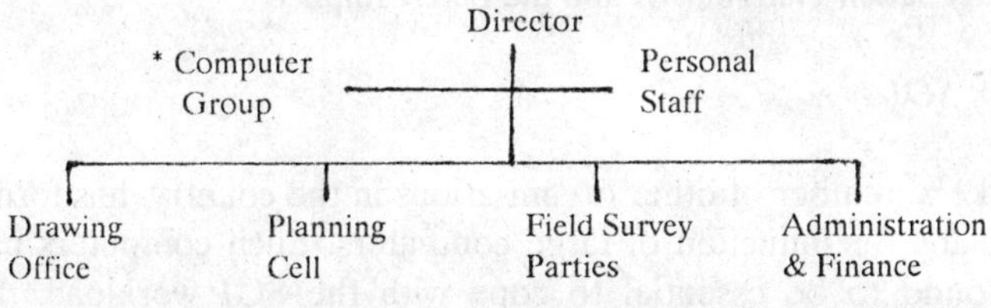

FIG. 16.3: Regional Circle After Computerisation
* Computer Group formed by taking 'Bright Boys' from other groups.

Importance Accorded to a Few

Because computer work demands people with above average intelligence, the Director is forced to choose the best from the various groups and put them in the Computer Group. By virtue of such relation, the members of this group tend to become 'elitist'.

Workload Not Shared By All

By the very nature of computer work, no sharing of workload is possible. In fact, it would be difficult for a person working in a field survey party to appreciate the problems, frustrations and constraints faced by a person working in a computer cell. Since most of the work engaged in by the computer cell is intellectual in nature, the 'computer boys' find it difficult to share such work. On the other hand, a person working in a field party may ask his colleague to do some part of a familiar work for some time and thus take time off as it were. Because of this phenomenon, non-computer departments tend to resent 'computer boys'.

Specialised Directorates

Computer work at the specialised directorate level demands access to large computers which the organisation does not have at present. Thus, the staff of specialised directorates are required to go to organisations (outside SOI) to process data. There has not been any major change in the structure of the specialised directorates due to use of computers. 'Bright Boys' of such directorates, however, are required to put in extra work compared to their colleagues.

Computerisation Plans of SOI and the Likely Impact

Plans of SOI

SOI, like a number of other organisations in the country, has formulated plans for induction of large computers. Such computers have been found to be essential to cope with the SOI workload. Implementation of these plans is beset with some problems. These are as follows:

(a) Non-availability of expertise in SOI.
(b) Need for creation of a computer group.
(c) Role of this Group *vis-a-vis* other groups.

Non-availability of Expertise in SOI

SOI is basically a surveying and mapping organisation. Therefore, it is not appropriate to expect SOI to possess expertise in computers. Though some members of staff of SOI have been trained on computers in foreign countries, such training has not been followed up seriously. Therefore, it has become necessary for SOI to think of recruiting experts to work with computers (when they are installed by SOI).

Recruitment of outside experts is beset with the following problems:

(a) Outsiders (if they are experts) would demand more pay and emoluments than SOI staff (who might be in the same age group and are likely to possess more experience in survey and mapping matters).
(b) Outsiders may be recruited on a contract basis.
(c) Computer staff tend to pass through the following stages of progress in the organisation (as depicted in Fig. 16.4).

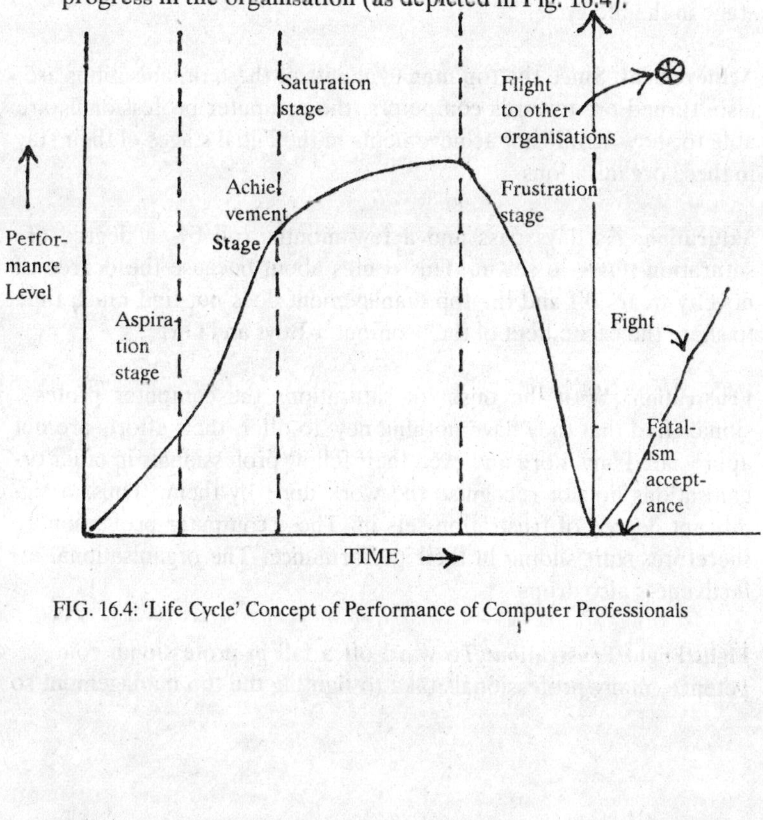

FIG. 16.4: 'Life Cycle' Concept of Performance of Computer Professionals

– Aspiration (hopes)	
– Achievement	
– Saturation	'Life Cycle' of progress
– Frustration	of Computer Experts
– Flight/Fatalism	

(d) Insiders resent prominence given to outsiders.

Stages in the 'Life Cycle' of Progress

Every organisation – large or small; Indian or multi-national; industrial or business; religious or military; academic or otherwise; governmental or non-governmental, tends to advertise for the best persons when it intends 'going computers'. Thus, a number of computer experts, in the hope of not only getting more emoluments than what they are hitherto getting but also contributing to professional calls of challenge, join these organisations. These professionals enter organisations with huge aspirations and hopes. Hence this is the first stage in the life cycle.

Achievement: Since the top managements of these organisations are also 'turned on' towards computers, the computer professionals are able to show significant achievements in the initial stages of their stay in these organisations.

Saturation: As days pass and a few months roll by, a degree of saturation tends to set in. This comes about because the degree of novelty wears off and the top management does not find much time to share the excitement of the 'Computer Boys and Girls'.

Frustration: With the onset of saturation, the computer professionals find that they have nothing new to offer, their efforts are not appreciated any more and even their fellow professionals in other organisations do not recognise the work done by them. Thus, a significant degree of frustration sets in. These computer professionals, therefore, start sliding in their performance. The organisational effectiveness also drops.

Fight/Flight/Frustration: To ward off a fall in professional competence, many professionals take to fighting the top management so that more job challenges are offered. Some professionals take to flight by looking for greener posts in other organisations. Those others who are not successful in either their fight or flight tend to accept their position in a fatalistic manner. These employees could at best be considered to be 'routine workers' with no new ideas to offer. Such workers would not find promotional avenues either, and are likely to stagnate.

Change in Structure

We have seen, so far, the impact of computers on the behaviour of persons engaged in computer work. Computers have an equal influence (if not more) on other components of the organisation and have a tendency to affect the performance of the various segments of the organisation.

New 'Power Centres'

As shown in Fig. 16.5, the 'Computer Division' or 'cell' concept conceptualised in the case of Survey of India (SOI), as in other large organisations, comes into existence when computers are introduced for the first time. These 'computer divisions' tend to become 'Power Centres' as they handle 'information'. In a way, Finance/Accounts departments on the one hand and Personal department on the other also have been handling sensitive information earlier. 'Computer Divisions' are able to store all information, whether sensitive or otherwise, in one central (and compact) place now. Thus, the 'power' of information is gradually getting shifted to 'computer professionals'.

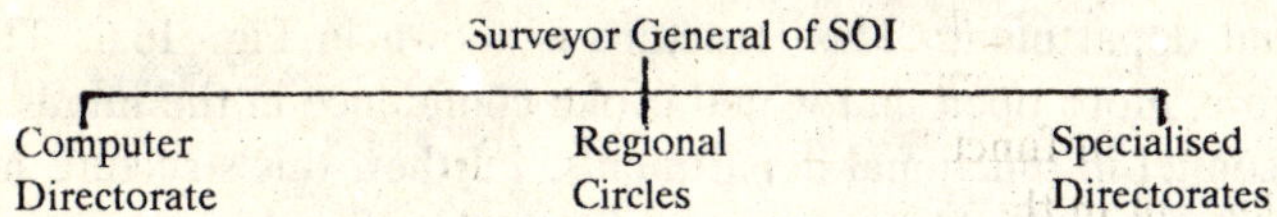

To plan, install, operate and control computer-based information. All computer personnel controlled from here.

FIG. 16.5: Centralised 'Computer Division'

Sense of Insecurity

The various employees (whether they are managerial, supervisory or otherwise) working in conventional departments find themselves 'left out', as it were. They are not able to understand the new equipment (computers) fast enough nor are they able to adapt themselves to new procedures and forms as a result of computerisation.

Types of Structures

There are basically two structures that emerge in any organisation 'going computers'. Of course, a third structure would also emerge, but this structure is peculiar to academic institutions and will be discussed separately.

Centralised Staff Structure

As shown in Fig. 16.5, all work related to computerisation is vested in the 'computer division'. The staff of the Computer Division work under the head of the Division. They may work with one functional department one day and with a completely strange department the very next day.

'Centralised Operations' and 'Distributed Staff'

In this structure, all planning, training and computer operations are handled by the computer division while development of information system is achieved by attaching computer professionals on a semi-permanent basis with the functional departments. The computer professionals, in effect, would be on the payroll of the concerned functional department. This structure is shown in Fig. 16.6. This structure is more open and would evoke confidence in the minds of the personnel in functional departments. Further, this structure has been tried out in the Government of India when financial advisers to various departments work in the concerned departments reporting to the Expenditure Secretary at the same time.

In this structure, computer personnel would have to report to 'two bosses' as it were. One boss would be the 'Technical Boss' at the Computer Division for technical matters, while the other would be the 'Functional/Operational Boss' at the functional division. This structure has been prevalent for a number of years in military organisations where the communications expert, engineering expert, ordinance expert, etc. were brought under command of the Force Commander. In order to ensure coordination with other friendly forces, these experts would also report to their technical bosses. This is more like a 'matrix structure' of orgnisation.

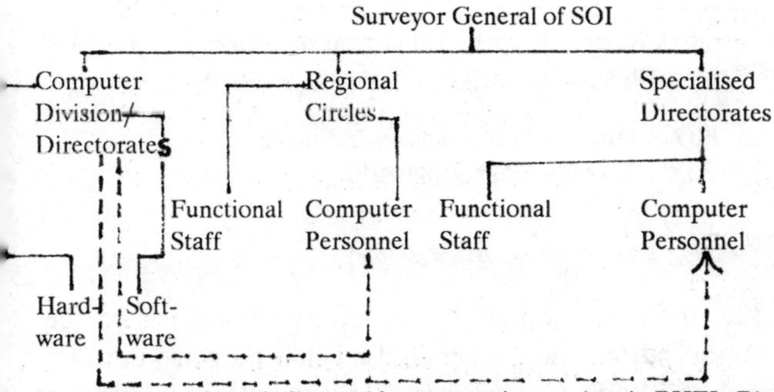

Note: A structure similar to this structure is prevalent in BHEL, Bhopal.

FIG. 16.6: 'Centralised Operations' and 'Distributed Staff' (a matrix structure?)

Structure in an Academic Environment

While we have seen various structures in a service organisation like SOI so far, it would be worthwhile to look at the structure that is found in an academic environment due to the advent of computers. This structure entails more freedom to the functional departments than that found in Fig. 16.6. In an organisation such as IIT or IISC, the various academic departments themselves are in a position to use computers without any large-scale help from the computer division. As shown in Fig. 16.7, only the hardware maintenance, software update and dissemination of information would be the responsibility of the computer division. Selection of tasks to be computerised, choice of software, maintenance of databases, etc. would be the responsibility of the computer division. This structure is more of a *laissez-faire* structure.

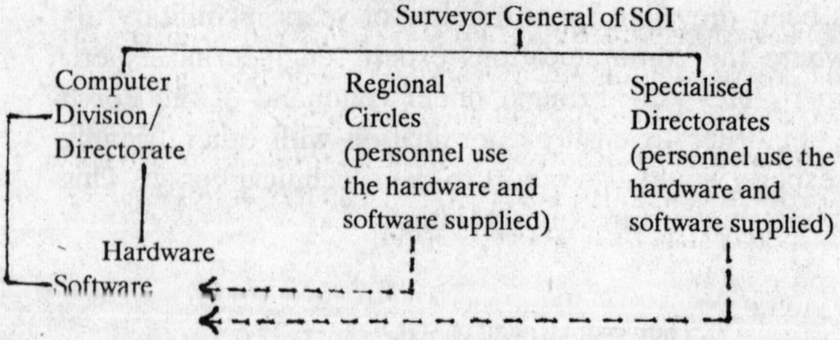

Note: On many occasions, functional department personnel become more proficient in computers as compared to personnel of computer divisions.

FIG. 7: Structure in an Academic Institution
(A *Laissez-faire* Approach)

Effect on Personnel

Whatever be the structure adopted, if computer professionals decide to stay in an organisation, they normally find that they are not in a position to reach the 'top'. Can we expect a computer professional who enters the computer division of the army to lead forces in a war? Can we expect a computer professional to head a police force when he would not know how to handle a prisoner or a riot? Thus, no organisation permits a computer professional to head it. If a computer professional wishes to reach the top, he is expected to branch off into a functional area during his 'junior management' or, at best, 'middle management' days.

Conclusion

An attempt has been made in this paper to analyse the various issues involved in the induction of computers in an organisation with special reference to organisational structures. A description of the merits and demerits of an 'endogenous' (in-house) as well as 'exogenous' (external) computer-professional group induction has also been tried. Since many organisations (whether they are large or small) do not encourage analysis of their structures in depth, it has not been attempted in this paper.

One can, however, see a clear emergence of 'Matrix' organisations with the advent of computers. One can also see the possibility of internal friction between the 'restraining forces' of the 'status-quoists' in the organisation and the 'driving forces' of the 'change-agents' in the organisation.

Computers are tools just like typewriters, photocopiers and the like with one major difference. Computers are 'active' in that they provide 'live' and 'hot' information.

The number of studies undertaken in the Indian context on the impact of computerisation on organisational structures need to be undertaken so that a systematic guideline could be evolved for use by organisations 'going computers'.

REFERENCES

CIER (1966). Data from 'State of the Information Processing Industry' prepared by CIER, 1966-1980.

Evans, C. (1979). *The Micro Millennium,* New York, 1979.

Myers, C.A. (Ed.) (1967). 'The Impact of Computerized Programs on Managers and Organization', an appendix in *The Impact of Computers on Managements,* the MIT Press, London, 1967.

Rathenau, G.W. (1982). 'The Impact of Information Technology on Social Organization', in Anderson, N.B. *et al.* (Eds.) *Information Society*, North-Holland Publishing Co., New York, 1982.

Vollebergh, J.J.A. (1981). *'Microprocessing and Microprogramming'*, 7(3), 1981.

17

COMPUTER LITERACY IN SCHOOLS

B. MAJUMDAR

The Computer Revolution

The electronic computer is the most fascinating invention of the later half of the present century. Like the industrial revolution, computer revolution is currently sweeping through our society causing deep and widespread changes in all the walks of human activity.

A digital computer is an electronic machine that processes data or facts at an astounding speed to produce useful information in the form of literals, numbers and graphics. The computer can store, retrieve, analyse and synthesise data or raw informations received from various sources to produce meaningful informations necessary in making decisions and solving problems.

Computers are increasingly being used in diverse areas such as business, education, publishing, medicine, household communication, etc. In business, the large volumes of accounting and record keeping data can be organised, stored and retrieved for specific purposes by the use of computers. Bills and statements can be processed and sent to customers in much less time and with much less effort. Planning and decision-making can be made fast and more accurate. In manufacturing process, computers are used to guide machine tools, direct production, control quality and monitor inventory levels. In modern offices, word processing helps to produce more accurate letters, reports and documents with much less effort. Automated filing uses far less storage space and enables workers to retrieve documents rapidly.

Fast and efficient record keeping in modern banking, hospitals, libraries and government activities have been facilitated by the use of computers. Instantaneous flight reservation from remote cities has become feasible due to the computers.

Computer has enabled the solution of complex scientific and engineering problems. Using computer, engineers are able to design products and simulate system performance which helps to avoid costly design error.

Growth of Computer Industry

The computer industry is growing very rapidly. With the advancement of semiconductor technology, computers are becoming less costly and more capable and reliable every year. Thus the 'microcomputers' of today are more powerful than the 'mainframe' computers of only a decade ago and offer greater capability, speed, storage and reliability. Rapid technological developments have also led to a significant reduction in the price of nearly all the computer components.

It is estimated that by 1987 the number of computers all over the world will have grown to 50 million, most of them being the small microcomputers. By 1993, there will be 170 million computers in the United States and about 70 per cent of the population will be using computer work-stations. According to the U.S. Bureau of Labour Statistics, five of the fastest-growing occupations within the next decade will be related to computers: computer service technicians, systems analyst, programmer, computer operator and equipment repair person.

Computer Literacy

The computer revolution is rapidly changing an industrial society to an information society in which the majority of labour force will be holding information-related jobs. Ignorance of computers will therefore render people functionally illiterate as does ignorance of reading, writing and arithmetic. These illiterates will not only be limited in their choice of careers, they will be isolated from a wealth of opportunities to gain information, new learning, social connections, entertainments, and so on. They will be denied use of the most powerful tool ever created for expanding the reach, creativity and intellectual potential of mankind. Professionals have therefore stressed the urgent need for teaching computer literacy in the schools.

Some schools of thought have, however, expressed reservation on the issue of computer literacy. There are those who argue that just as people no longer need to know anything about how automobiles or televisions work in order to use them, children need not learn how computers work. Some people suspect that commercial interests lie behind the pressure to place computers in classrooms and agree that all students need not be 'computer literate'. Others fear that computers will dehumanize education and lead to a further erosion of basic skills.

Meaning of Computer Literacy

The concept of computer 'literacy' is so new that there is no general agreement on its definition. Some authorities emphasise computer awareness, or becoming knowledgeable about the effect of computers on our lives and our society.

> Computer literacy is 'an awareness and understanding of the computer, its role in society, and its impact on education' (Holly O'Donnell)

Others suggest that true computer literacy can only be achieved through the learning of computer programming to control the computer;

> "If you can tell the computer how to do the things you want to, you are computer literate." (Arthur Leuhrmann)

Some other experts advocate using the computer as a tool in many ways and suggest that full literacy must be comprehensive in scope:

> "Not only programming, computer literacy should include the use of information retrieval, word processing, statistics, and other application systems." (David Moursund)

> "The ability to use suitably programmed computers in appropriate ways in accomplishing tasks and solving problems and ability to make informed judgements about social and ethical issues involving computer and communication systems." (Beverly Hunter)

> "Computer literacy is 'whatever understanding, skills, and at-

titudes one needs to function effectively within a given social role that directly or indirectly involves computers'." (Ronald Anderson and Daniel Klassen)

As these definitions indicate, there is no general agreement, even among experts, regarding the objectives of computer literacy. The main point is that computers will be used in all areas of society, including education. The task for the educators is to decide the type and level of use that will improve education for children.

Computer Literacy Pilot Project

Computer literacy has been introduced in the elementary and middle schools in many developed countries. Many colleges are including minimal computer literacy as a requirement for graduation. The Ministry of Education of the Government of India has introduced in 1984 a pilot project for Computer Literacy and Studies in Schools (CLASS) at the secondary and higher secondary level. The programme, in the first phase, is to fulfil the following objectives:

(a) Provide students with a broad understanding of computers and their use.
(b) Familiarise students with the range of computer applications in all walks of human activity and the potentiality of the computer as an information processing tool.
(c) Demystify computers and develop a degree of ease and familiarity with computers which would be conducive to developing individual creativity in identifying and developing applications relevant to the immediate environment of the child.

In the first year of the pilot scheme, 250 schools were identified for participation. The scheme has been extended to another 1,000 schools in 1985 and 1986. The schools have been attached to 50 Resource Centres spread all over the country. Some of the important functions identified for these centres are:

- Training and Support/Consultancy assistance to teachers of the selected schools;
- Monitoring and implementation of the programme;
- Maintenance of the computers with the assistance of Computer

Maintenance Corporation;
- Development of curricula and teaching strategies;
- Software development, both for computer literacy as well as computer assisted instruction/learning;
- Promotional activity with a view to popularising the programme.

The Government is providing the necessary infrastructure for implementing the pilot project. The experience gained in the pilot phase will be highly useful at the stage of the subsequent wider implementation of the scheme.

Conclusion

Computer can be used as a versatile audio-visual teaching machine right from the elementary school level. Computer-assisted instruction can virtually replace a tutor by a computer for imparting education. The computer is used to provide information and motivate learning through the use of graphics and animation. The intention is not to replace the teacher but to enhance the ability of the teacher to teach more effectively. The successful implementation of computer literacy and education on such a wide scale will, however, depend on the indigenous manufacture of micro-computer system at low cast, development and availability of proper CAI softwares and the use of regional languages in computer education.

REFERENCES

CLASS (1984). Report of the National Workshop on Computer Literacy Curriculum held at NCERT on 26-27 March, NCERT.

Clements, Douglas H. (1985). *Computers in Early and Primary Education,* Prentice-Hall.

Fuori, William M. and Aufiero, Lawrence J. (1986). *Computers and Information Processing,* Prentice-Hall.

Goldstein, Larry Joel (1986). *Computers and Their Applications*, Prentice-Hall, 1986.

Riedesel, C. Alan and Clements, Douglas H. (1985). *Coping with Computers in the Elementary and Middle Schools,* Prentice-Hall.

18

ORGANISATIONAL SET-UP OF COMPUTER EDUCATION IN UNIVERSITIES

RAMANA REDDY

Introduction

The use of information technology is expanding very rapidly in all walks of life. The recent advances in microprocessor technology have resulted in a second industrial revolution. Our society too cannot escape the influence of this phenomenon due to its all pervasive nature. It is therefore essential that our society should be able to face and benefit from this revolution.

These developments will also have their impact on the speed of communication, utilisation of resources and quality of decision-making, not only in business and industrial organisations, but also in various departments and sections of universities and governments. In this context, one major concern to be faced is the acute shortage of trained manpower to implement various computer projects. It is of utmost importance that the youth of our country keeps pace with advancing technology and, therefore, computer education must be imparted to a much wider circle of students.

In spreading this computer culture, the universities have a lot of obligation to the society. In right earnest, the universities must introduce a number of computer courses in a big way.

This paper deals briefly with the role of computers in Education and Organisational set-up for the introduction of Computer Courses in Universities in exploiting the unlimited potentialities of computers in various fields. Also several manpower computer training programmes in vogue are presented.

Application of Computers in Universities

Computers have ingressed into all walks of life — medical, health, engineering, manufacturing, space exploration, administration, education, etc., in fact, any field of application. In a university environment, they find immediate application in areas such as:

- Various stages of processing related to examination
- Payroll
- Financial Accounting
- Integrated Development Works
- Libraries
- Correspondence Courses and Continuing Education
- Education and Training

Education and Training

The utility of computers in the field of Education and Training is discussed in this section out of the several applications listed above. Computer will act as an aid, but also act as a companion and provide an interactive means of learning. Computer technologies when used with forethought, could provide powerful aids to the classroom and can be considered as a good teacher.

Computer Aided Learning (CAL), Intelligent Computer Aided Instruction (ICAI) and Computer Based Training (CBT) are revolutionising every facet of education and training. Computers are now used in an interactive mode to promote and reinforce the process of learning. With the aid of computers, course material is presented, problems are posed and practice is given at the learner's own pace and level of understanding and assimilation. Thus, a student is benefited in a number of ways. Simultaneously, the teacher and the institution concerned also derive benefits by the :

- standardisation of teaching material and integration of curricula
- result-oriented teaching through a variety of modes, including graphic presentation, simulation exercises, quiz programs, etc.
- increased duration of instruction without corresponding increase in teaching hours
- easy simulation of situations

- professional education at reduced costs
- timely introduction of emerging and advanced technology
- extension programs to remote locations

Thus, imparting education and instruction becomes more effective both qualitatively and quantitatively, being qualitative- and quantitative-wise.

Computer Education in University

A university should have a clearly stated policy framework to impart computer education at various levels for people with different levels of background. To effectively meet the various requirements of government, industry, collegiate and school level education, the organisational set-up of computer education in a university may be as follows. This structure is based on the facts: (i) there is an acute shortage of trained manpower, and (ii) the computer facilities are expensive and scarce. Hence these points should be borne in mind in planning computer projects in a university.

Organisational Structure

For our Indian conditions, various computer courses that can be offered are:

1. Computer Engineering:

   (a) 4-year B. Tech. (10+2 level background)
   (b) 3-year B. Tech. (Post B.Sc/B.A.)
   (c) M. Tech. (for successful candidates through GATE)

2. Computer Applications:

   (a) 3-year Master of Computer Applications – MCA (Post B.Sc/B.A./B.Com./B.Tech.)
   (b) 1-year (Post B.Sc/B.A./B.Com. – Maths background)
   (c) 1-year PG DCA (Post-Graduate Diploma in Computer Applications for students without Maths background)

3. Continuing and Correspondence Courses:

   (a) Short-term Certificate Courses in Computer Languages
   (b) Evening/Part-time Diploma Courses as specified under 2(b) and 2(c)
   (c) Correspondence Courses in (a) and (b) cited above

4. Computer Centre:

   (a) To meet the computational requirements of various computer courses proposed;
   (b) To cater to the computer requirements of students, research scholars and research schemes and projects of various departments in the university; and
   (c) To carry out consultancy work of private and governmental agencies.

As the computational facilities are expensive and they require special maintenance and also due to paucity of resources, all of them should be maintained at one place — called Computer Centre. Of course, terminals (intelligent and dummy type) can be provided in various needy departments. Also the trained manpower should be used flexibly for teaching various courses. The equipment should not get duplicated. All these things are possible if the various sections, 1 to 4 proposed above, are brought under one umbrella, namely school of computer science and engineering. The organisational set-up of computer education discussed above is shown in Fig. 18.1.

Proposals for Faculty Generation

Teacher performance is the most crucial input in the field of education and training. Whatever be the course design and resources provided, in the ultimate analysis these have to be interpreted and implemented by teachers.

Since the linkage of technical education with growing manpower requirements of the computer industry has remained weak, adequate training facilities have not been introduced in the educational institutions. This has resulted not only in acute shortage of manpower for industry, but also in a paucity of trained teachers for educational institutions. Even those who undergo formal training do not look upon the teaching profession as a desirable career option in terms of remuneration as well as status.

To obviate the above limitations, the Department of Education and Department of Electronics, Government of India, have already started a number of training programmes at several institutions and universities. Briefly, the training programmes are:

- One year reorientation/cross-migration course for fresh Ph.D's in Mathematics, Statistics, Physics or Engineering.
- Retraining of existing teachers from Mathematics, Physics and Engineering disciplines to enable them to become Computer Science teachers. These courses are of one year duration.
- A modular training program for the existing teachers. A number of modules are designed to suit current requirements. Each of these modules are of 4-8 weeks duration and are offered during vacations.

Further, it is recommended that teachers of computer courses be given suitable incentives so that talented people are attracted.

SCHOOL/DEPARTMENT OF COMPUTER SCIENCE AND ENGINEERING

Section/Dept. 1	*Section/Dept. 2*	*Section/Dept. 3*	*Section/Dept. 4*
1. 4-yr B.Tech. program (Post 10+2)	1. 3-yr MCA program (Post B.Sc/ B.Com/B.A.)	1. Distance Education 2. Short-term Certificate courses	1. Computer Centre (Consisting computing facilities for all courses and programmes
2. 3-yr B. Tech. (Post B.Sc./ B.A.) 3. M.Tech. program	2. 1-yr DCA program (Post B.Sc/ B.Com/B.A. with mathematics background 3. 1-yr DCA program (Post-graduate diploma for students without mathematics background)	3. Part-time/ evening classes in DCA 4. Training programs	2. Consultancy works

FIG. 18.1: Organizational Set-Up of Various Computer Courses in a University

Conclusions

The philosophy and the need of computers in the modern context are discussed. The obligation of a university in fulfilling the requirements of the society are presented. The role of computer in a university environment is described and its particular contribution as a tool for imparting education and teaching has been brought out briefly.

An organisational set-up of computer education in a university is suggested to optimally utilise the limited trained manpower and the expensive and scarce computer facilities. Also, the various manpower training programs introduced by the Government of India are given.

Unlimited potential of computers should be exploited for our educational purposes which, in turn, will boost computer based industry and quality production.

REFERENCES

Ashok, A.G. (1986). 'The Role of Computers in Education', *Ibid.*, pp. 129-132.

Pulkesi, M. (1986). 'Use of Computers in Teaching', *Ibid.*, pp. 85-90.

Report of the Expert Group on Computer Education and Training (1986). Government of Andhra Pradesh.

Report of the Working Group on Evolving Strategy for Teachers' Training for Implementing Computer Education Programmes (1986). Department of Electronics, Government of India.

Sanwal, Mukul (1986). 'Microcomputer Applications for Development Administration: The Strategic Significance', National Conference on computers and the Society, Annamalai University, pp. 13-21.

Sarukesi (1986). 'Computers in Education'; CSI National Conference of Business and Industry Group held at Coimbatore, December 12 and 13, 1986, pp. 32-34.

19

COMPUTER MANPOWER DEVELOPMENT: Indian Scene

P.G. REDDY

Introduction

Information explosion is the most important phenomenon that has had the greatest impact on humanity during this decade. The rapid strides in the area of micro electronics and the space programme have been the genesis of this phenomenon. The latest technological innovations in terms of data sensing, signal processing, fast data capture, storage, data retrieval, world-wide communications, developments in display technology, artificial intelligence, and knowledge based systems are the features that have contributed specifically towards this information explosion. However, all these are either directly or indirectly dependent on computer technology.

The fact that computer is a very powerful tool in information processing and that it relieves the intelligent human being from the monotonous and time-consuming task so as to concentrate his efforts in the most important areas of problem identification and decision-making has been fully realised, and in all walks of life there seems to be an unspoken urgency in harnessing this powerful tool in the general upliftment of the nation and the people in general. Computers have made their impact in all walks of life.

Computers and Education

This explosive growth of computer technology during the last half of this century has been driven, in part, by contributions from institutions of higher education. But just as education has contributed to the growth of the computer field, computer technology has influenced all phases of education. The computer field has matured to the point that most of us accept computers as a normal part of our professional lives. However, the impact of advances in computer technology on education and the educational process is just starting to be realised.

Early computer applications were often labour intensive. A large number of computer operators, programmers and other computer professionals were typically found at most installations, and the average computer user was convinced that only a skilled programmer could provide the software needed to implement even the simplest application. As micro-processor and integrated circuit technology developed, many of the hardware barriers to computer accessibility were removed. The consequence of this development is that the computer user is able to directly interact with the computer system without the assistance of a skilled programmer. Thus, software rather than hardware, emerges as the limiting factor in a number of applications. Data Base Systems, Word-processing Systems, Spread Sheet Programs, and similar application programmes overcome many limitations, allowing a wide range of non-computer experts (those without computer-programming or computer-technology skills) to effecitvely use a computer system. These software advances have significantly affected the educational needs of both those wishing to enter the computer area and those expecting to use computers as tools in a different career path. The demand for computer operators, entry-level data processing personnel, and beginning programmers is well below the number being turned out. On the other hand, the number of skilled computer technicians, computer engineers, software engineers, and similar computer professionals is far below current needs.

An even interesting trend is developing in other professional areas as computers are introduced into other fields. A major demand is developing for courses directed at applying computer techniques to specific application and problem areas. Students taking these courses are interested in understanding how computer techniques and tools that support various applications can be used as part of the problem-solving process. In the face of increasingly varied user demands and constantly changing technology, it is nearly impossible to predict the need for graudates from different programmes of study.

Impact of Technology on Education

With the development of microcomputers and with the cost of the systems coming down, it is essential that every college should be provided with a computer facility. Students studying in all fields will have access to these computer facilities with essentially unlimited memory, intelligent software, and interactive graphics. This capability will impact the educational process in a positive manner.

The Government is emphasising the use of the computer tool in optimal utilisation of its resources. It is also keen to use this tool for mass education reaching the rural masses. Like all tools, this also needs an intelligent person to handle it, and so we come to our problem.

Manpower Requirements

As already mentioned, the major problem facing the country today is the non-availability of trained manpower in this area. This immediately focuses the attention on computer literacy and facilities to educate and train large numbers of personnel in this critical area. The Department of Electronics and UGC is greatly seized with this problem and had set up a joint panel under the chairmanship of Professor V. Rajaraman, under whose recommendations several programmes were introduced. The manpower panel report has brought home the inadequacies of the manpower resources.

However, that report is already outdated. It is necessary to take a fresh look at our present manpower requirements in view of the changed scene in the country as also the rapid development in hardware and falling in prices. In addition, the Government of India's recent liberal policy for generating software for software export purposes.

The methodology adopted for estimating manpower requirements is as follows. The total demand for computer professionals was estimated by assuming certain minimum personnel requirements for each installation in a particular class of computer. Given the projected number of computer installations, it was possible therefore to arrive at the number of personnel required, at different skill/hierarchical levels, for all the computer installations projected over the Seventh Plan Period.

Certain minimum qualifications were assumed at each

hierarchical/skill level and based on these, the qualification-wise break-up of professionals over five years was arrived at. Thus these figures provide qualification-wise projections of national manpower demand. From the qualification-wise figures, the number of teachers required for each of these courses, appropriate teacher-student ratios, similar to those suggested by the DOE/UGC report were arrived at. The projected hardware growth for the Seventh Plan Period is shown in Table 19.1.

TABLE 19.1: Projected Hardware Growth up to 1990 (Seventh Plan Period)

Category	Year					
	1985-86	1986-87	1987-88	1988-89	1989-90	Total
MICRO/PC	10,000	15,000	22,000	31,000	42,000	120,000
MINI	500	750	1,000	1,250	1,500	5,000
MAINFRAME	50	100	150	200	250	750
SUPER COMPUTER	—	—	20	—	—	20

The computer industry, for purposes of convenience, has been usually classified under the following three major categories:

(i) hardware manufacturing;
(ii) software industry; and
(iii) user organisations.

These sectors need personnel, not only with computer science knowledge, but also with knowledge of application areas, together with capabilities in systems analysis and design. The manufacturing units also need hardware engineers with sufficient knowledge and skill in maintaining hardware systems. The recent reduction in cost of small computers, coupled with enhanced software features, has made it possible for these machines to be used profitably by very small business houses. Such installations require computer professionals who could provide the users with total support service in terms of computer applications, software development and routine maintenance.

The computerisation effort, considering all levels of application, has to address the training of the following categories of computer professionals:

1. Managers
2. Systems Analysts
3. Programmers
4. Computer Operators
5. Data Entry Operators
6. Small Systems Managers
7. Hardware Engineers
8. Computer Teachers
9. Computer Researchers and Scientists

As per the job requirements and the standard patterns of education available in the country, the following qualifications are required for personnel to be utilized at the user installations (Table 19.2).

TABLE 19.2: Required Qualifications of Personnel at User Installations

Designation	CATEGORY			
	Super Computer	Main Frame	Mini	Micro/PC
Managers & above	M. Tech., MBA	M. Tech. B. Tech.	M. Tech. B. Tech.	—
Systems Analysts	M. Tech., B. Tech MCA	B. Tech. MCA	MCA DCA (PG)	—
Programmers	DCA (PG)	DCA (PD)	B. Sc. (Comp.)	
Computer Operators		I.T.I. Certificate		
Data Entry Operators		I.T.I. Certificate		
Small System Manager				B.Sc.(Comp.)

Table 19.3 gives the estimated number of personnel required for one unit of each type of computer, whereas Table 19.4 illustrates the basis for calculation of required hardware engineers. From the above assumption, Table 19.5 shows the estimated figures of computer professionals required at the national level by category and by qualification (Table 19.6) for the Seventh Plan Period.

TABLE 19.3: Estimated Number of Personnel Required for One Unit of each Type of Computer

Designation	CATEGORY			
	Super Computer	Main Frame	Mini	Micro/PC
Managers and above	3	2	1	—
Systems Analysts	20	5	2	—
Programmers	30	15	3	—
Computer Operators	10	5	2	—
Data Entry Operators	50	20	5	1
Small System Managers	—	—	—	—

TABLE 19.4: Basis for Calculation of Requirement of Hardware Engineers

Category of Computer	Designation/Qualification	
	Senior Hardware Engineer (B. Tech.)	Junior Hardware Engineer (D.C.E.)
Super Computer	3 per unit	5 per unit
Main frame	1 per unit	2 per unit
Mini	1 per 10 units	1 per 5 units
Micro/PC	1 per 100 units	1 per 50 units

While it is important to introduce professional computer courses in the formal education system as early as possible, the retraining of the active workforce must not be overlooked. Many job profiles are changed because of the introduction of hi-tech equipment like computers. It is not always desirable to fill the new job positions with new people. The persons who have worked in a given position/application for a number of years would have gained valuable job experience which, combined with software knowledge, would form an important asset to the organisation. The computer training of the in-service population should therefore form an important component of the computer education policy.

TABLE 19.5: Requirement of Computer Professionals (All India Level)

Category	Year					
	1985-86	1986-87	1987-88	1988-89	1989-90	Total
Managers and above	600	950	1,360	1,650	2,000	6,560
Systems Analysts	1,250	2,000	3,150	3,500	4,250	14,150
Programmers	2,250	3,750	5,850	6,750	8,250	26,850
Computer Operators	1,250	2,000	2,950	3,500	4,250	13,950
Data Entry Operators	13,500	20,750	31,000	41,250	54,500	161,000
Small Systems Managers	10,000	15,000	22,000	31,000	42,000	120,000

TABLE 19.6: Projected National Manpower Demand

Qualification	Year					
	1985-86	1986-87	1987-88	1988 89	1989-90	Total
M. Tech.	300	475	810	825	1,000	3,410
B. Tech.	600 (200)	1,000 (325)	1,580 (530)	1,860 (635)	2,320 (820)	7,360 (2,510)
M.C.A.	650	1,050	1,650	1,850	2,250	7,450
D.C.A. (PG)	1,250	2,000	2,950	3,500	4,250	13,950
B. Sc. (computers)	10,750	16,250	23,950	33,250	44,750	128,950
D.C.E.	400	650	1,040	1,270	1,640	5,000
D.C.A. (PD)	750	1,250	1,950	2,250	2,750	8,950
I.T.I. Certificate	14,750	22,750	33,950	44,750	58,750	174,950

* This figure includes the estimated requirement (in parantheses) of the computer manufacturing industry for hardware maintenance personnel.

Resources for Training

Three important resources for imparting training in this area are:

- Computer Hardware
- Teachers
- Software

Since a major part of the training is skill oriented, a greater emphasis should be given to the practical training (hands-on experience) in all courses. Although some of the centres which are currently running the programs have facilities for such training, they should be considerably augmented for providing adequate practical experience.

With regard to teachers, the paucity of trained faculty causes serious problems in starting various programmes/courses. The teachers available at present are not only inadequate in terms of number, but also lack adequate formal training. It is needless to say that there should be an immediate emphasis on teacher training programmes so as to meet not only the teacher requirements but also to ensure high standard of computer education.

Teachers Requirement

The estimated teachers requirement for manpower generation are given in Tables 19.8 and 19.9. These figures have been derived using the teacher-student ratios shown in Table 19.7. The total number of teachers at various levels required exceeds 20,000 over the Seventh Plan Period.

TABLE 19.7: Teacher-Student Ratios assumed for Calculating Faculty Requirement

Qualification/Course	Teacher-Student Ratio
M. Tech.	1 : 4
B. Tech.	1 : 10
M.C.A.	1 : 10
D.C.A. (PG)	1 : 10
B. Sc. (Computers)	1 : 20*
D.C.E.	1 : 10
D.C.A. (PD)	1 : 10
I.T.I. (Certificate	1 : 20

* This reduction in teacher-student ratio is due to the assumption that only one-third of the students will be related to the computer area.

TABLE 19.8: Estimated Requirement of Teachers for Various Courses

Course for which Teachers Required	Year					Total
	1985-86	1986-87	1987-88	1988-89	1989-90	
M. Tech.	80	120	200	210	250	860
B. Tech.	800	130	200	230	290	930
M.C.A.	80	130	210	230	280	930
D.C.A. (PG)	160	250	370	440	530	1,750
B.Sc. (Comp.)	540	810	1,200	1,660	2,240	6,450
D.C.E.	50	80	130	160	210	630
D.C.A. (PD)	90	150	240	280	340	1,100
I.T.I.(Cert.)	740	1,140	1,700	2,240	2,940	8,760

TABLE 19.9: Level-wise Requirement of Faculty at Different Categories of Institutions

Faculty	Year					Total
	1985-86	1986-87	1987-88	1988-89	1989-90	
University						
Professors	30	50	90	100	120	400
Readers	60	110	180	200	240	810
Lecturers	140	180	270	300	370	1220
Lab. Instructors/ Tutors/Demonstrators	170	290	440	510	620	2040
Degree College						
Professors	50	70	110	150	200	580
Readers	100	150	220	300	210	1170
Lecturers	150	220	330	460	610	1760
Lab. Instructors/ Tutors/Demonstrators	240	370	540	750	1020	2940
Polytechnic						
Head	10	20	30	40	50	150
Lecturers	20	40	60	80	100	300
Assistant Lecturers	40	60	100	120	150	470
Lab. Instructors/ Tutors/Demonstrators	70	110	180	200	250	810
I.T.I.						
Head	120	170	260	340	450	1330
Lecturers	230	340	520	680	900	2650
Assistant Lecturers	310	510	770	1020	1340	3980
Lab. Instructors/ Tutors/Demonstrators	570	880	1280	1690	2210	6630

Manpower Requirement for Software Export

In addition to that shown in Table 19.9, there will be some more professionals required for software export. The Government of India has set up a target of Rs. 300 crores p.a. for software exports to be achieved by 1990. Quite recently (December 1986), the Department of Electronics (DOE) has announced several incentives for generating software for export purpose and also debated the issue of setting up of a chain of Indian Institutes of Information Technology (IITs) for generating the manpower needed in Computer Science area. If this target is to be met, and this is not impossible, then we need to gear up now, take a stock of resources, plan a line of action to meet the target. Low manpower cost is to our advantage, but we also have to establish our credibility. As is true for any other industry, a strong local market must exist before export is possible. The export market cannot be just aimed till a national market exists to absorb the export surplus. No doubt the Government in its new liberal computer policy has provided enough incentives for software export, but it is looking abroad for its own software requirements, e.g. the software needed by the banking industry or the software needed by the Indian Railways for freight movement.

Manpower Shortage

TABLE 19.10: Estimated Availability of Manpower

Qualification	1985-86	1986-87	1987-88	1988-89	1989-90	Total
M. Tech.	265	270	270	270	270	1345
B. Tech.	345	605	605	605	605	2855
M.C.A.	30	180	420	420	420	1890
DCA (PG)	660	840	840	840	840	4020
DCA (PD)	480	480	480	480	480	2400

Ph.D.	Projected Requirement	Available
1980-85	250	60
1985-90	450	?

From Table 19.10, we have clearly established that there is a need for a large number of computer trained manpower. The dearth of manpower in the area of computer science is universal. All forecasts made have been underestimates and our manpower shortage has been persistent. With the paucity of trained manpower at various levels and non-availability of appropriate training programmes, small private training centres have mushroomed all over the country. These, of course, are at least interested in training. They are, after all, only out to collect money. While developing manpower, attention must be paid to all apsects of training, including computer facilities management. There is a scramble for acquiring hardware, little realising what they are letting themselves in for. A proper functional structure has to be set up within the organisation. The staff needs training in the use of machine and the maintenance of the software.

Resources for the Manpower Development

Manpower development calls for a major commitment on account of:

- substantial capital investments
- setting up standards for training and material
- setting up panels to review the training being given and
- setting up panels to monitor the resources provided and augmented.

Before we dwell on the above points, there is a major crisis in training – the faculty needed to teach the growing number of students are preferring, understandably, to enter industry with higher salaries and incentives. This results in a two-fold problem of not enough graduates with advanced degrees and not enough faculty to provide computer education. This is a classic example of 'eating the seed corn'.

Who should pay for the manpower cost? And how should the computer culture be spread?

In manpower development, the Government must play a major role by providing adequate support to the educational institutions apart from setting up its own.

Computer Education

University Sector

A number of institutions/universities have Computer Science and

Engineering programs (CSE) ranging from M. Tech., B. Tech., M.C.A. and D.C.A. programmes. In some cases, programmes have been established in independent departments, while in other cases, new programmes have been established within the existing departments and operate parallel with the host programme. This category is very less. In most of the institutions at present, only partial CSE programmes exist as options of Electrical Engineering and Electronics and Communication Engineering. Most of the programmes operate in their own way and there are no standards being set nor followed. There is no Accreditation Board for Computer Science and Engineering, and even the AICTE, which has no full-time members from Computer Science, has been dealing with this subject in a very tardy manner. There are, in most cases, no resources necessary for CSE programmes commensurate with other engineering and science programmes at the institution. However, the rapid pace of developments in the computer field places severe strains on laboratory resources. Keeping equipment resources current is a problem that may be more severe in CSE programmes than in other engineering and science programmes.

While partial programmes that are options within electrical or electronics engineering or other programmes share many of the needs of complete programmes, they usually have their own unique set of problems. In many cases, the faculty responsible for the option will have their degrees and most of their professional experience in the field of the main programme. Their expertise may not completely span the breadth of the CSE field. Consequently, the optional curriculum will not be comprehensive. Naturally, the option shares the resources of the host programme. In almost all cases this exacerbates the problem of expanding and keeping equipment and other resources current.

Very new or projected programmes also have their own unique needs. In many cases, there are initially few or no faculty and/or administrators with expertise in the field. Therefore the expertise to develop a curriculum in the area may initially be missing and the original faculty and administrators may lack knowledge of the faculty expertise and resources needed to establish a CSE programme.

As already mentioned, these new programmes need special funding for development of resources needed. UGC (University Grants Commission)/DOE (Department of Electronics) and Government of India are encouraging the development of CSE programmes in

Institutions. Even though adequate funding is provided for starting these programmes, they are still to address themselves and build up an organisation to oversee and advise the institutions about the development of CSE programmes. Many of these funding agencies, even though started in an earnest way in the beginning for CSE programmes development, have been satisfied and relieved of their responsibilities the moment they provide funds and only satisfied with utilisation certificates from the organisations. Some of these funding organisations, of late, have started interfering in the purchase of the computers and/or freely advocate (unsolicited) the mini and micro computers for CSE programmes. This aspect has not only delayed the process of establishing CSE programmes but in many cases it has a snowballing effect in the negative directions. Institutions, as they are in this country, with several funding agencies have been finding it difficult to start any new programmes like CSE programmes and hence in many cases remain content in establishment of a computer centre with a mini or a micro computer with or without staff.

It is a common observation that in most of the places the computers are hardly ever used for more than two hours per day when they are installed, and at any rate most of the university computer centres are not being used beyond one shift for several reasons.

Even though the manpower committee debated all these issues and also gave several suggestions, Government of India and UGC have not established any committee or a body to implement the CSE programme. Hence, we suggest the Accreditation Board for Computer Science and Engineering (ABCSE) should be establihsed either by the UGC or by the Government of India whose objectives would be to establish accreditation criteria for programmes in the computer area. The committee task would be to address all aspects of CSE programme – curriculum, faculty, and resources – and established the following overall goals for the model programme in CSE project:

- provide an overview of the desirable features of graduate and undergraduate academic programs in computer area;
- provide a standard of comparison to guide the development of new programmes or modify and upgrade established programmes;
- provide an interpreation of ABCSE criteria for minimum

programme standards;
- establish a set of standards that can be used to design 'Target of Excellence' programmes;
- define the CSE aspects of a curriculum in a manner that allows flexibility to meet the requirements of individual institutions;
- provide guidance to academic administrators concerning the level of commitment needed to support a programme.

The academic institutions such as the universities and IITs will have to play their role, not merely teaching, training or research. Yes, they must do that. But they must do more practical things; maybe in hardware modification, maybe in modifying systems software or developing general purpose application packages. All this activity should be able to generate financial resources for these institutions. How about a university owned company? Why should business activity be done by the private sector or the state sector? The universities in Britain have realised the importance of this kind of activity, perhaps out of necessity when the British Government imposed massive cuts on allocation to the universities in 1981. It was a question of survival for some of the smaller universities, say like Salford. The more enterprising managed to prosper by setting up companies abandoning pure, abstract research for some time when attention was concentrated on generating resources. The Government philosophy in Britain at that time was and even today is that 'the schools had to understand the need to create wealth before spending it'. The University of Salford, for example, exploits all its software developments through a company called 'Salford University Industrial Centre Ltd.'.

Computer Education at College and Pre-College Level Education

We had discussed already about the need of having CSE courses at Institutions/Universities level which generates M. Tech's, B. Tech's, MCA's, etc. Apart from these highly qualified people, we also need persons to do more mundane jobs and they certainly need not spend a long number of years to get degrees like M. Tech. If you look at the M. Tech's, you will find that a majority of them are busy doing routine commercial jobs for which the long years spent on education are a complete waste. Why can't we introduce training for young persons, boys and girls, just after completing their 12th standard, i.e. after +2 stage. Introduction of computers at college level will greatly help to generate manpower needed at lower levels.

With the advent of personal computers (PC), it is quite possible now that computers could be made available to colleges and schools so as to familiarise the use of computers. What would be the impact of the personal computer on the educational process is very difficult to imagine, but we do have a few clues as to what may occur. Just as the calculator replaced the slide rule in engineering and science courses, the PC will replace the calculator. Its potention in education, however, is much more than simply being a better tool to do the same job.

Advantages

Some important advantages of the computer in education are evident now. For example, when a student is asked to solve a problem involving a large amount of calculation, the process of performing the calculations becomes the focus of the lesson. That is, the student studies the theory, organises the problem to be solved, and then begins the calculation. At that point, the process of operating the calculator becomes more important to the student. Consequently, the true lesson is lost to the task of pushing calculator buttons. If the student is asked to perform the same problem as a computer, the solution takes a different form. The student organises the theory in the language of the computer; a language much like the equations of the theory. Therefore, the student's efforts towards obtaining the calculation actually take the form of rewriting and rethinking the theory of the problem. The computer is then the one that must focus on obtaining the actual solution. A student who can instruct a computer how to solve a problem has a good grasp of the problem.

Another benefit of computer use is that computer simulations can be useful and effective teaching tools. The computer can aid the student in obtaining more insight into the scientific principles being studied. Once a student has obtained a solution to a problem calculated by computer, very little effort is involved in obtaining more solutions to the same problem using differing input. The ability to obtain many solutions to a problem in a matter of a few minutes can provide the student with intuition about the subject matter – intuition generally not possible without a computer. If a solution to a problem is represented in an easily understood form, such as graphcially, a student can learn much about subject matter by changing parameters and seeing the effect on the result.

The computer can, in many cases, be a substitute for laboratory experiments, like physics and chemistry, at the introductory level. The personal computers can provide, in simulated form, much of the information that is gained in the laboratories. Finally, the computer can demonstrate principles that are difficult to present in a lecture form. Lectures can be supplemented with programmes prepared by the course instructors that would demonstrate the fundamentals of the lecture subject matter. These programmes, which could use graphic forms, would allow the student to gain more insight into the subject matter.

The introduction of personal computers into the educational process is sometimes equated with a large faculty effort to produce computer-assisted instruction. If the goal is to teach students using the computer as a delivery medium, then a very large effort will be required to produce 'course ware'.

Computers in Teaching

Computers can be used to deliver instruction in a variety of ways. These applications, sometimes called computer-assisted instruction or computer-augmented learning, include drill and practice – the reason most elementary schools buy computers – as well as tutorials, instructional support tools, and environmental simulations.

The computer can support the instructional process in a number of other ways. For example, computers can be used in the science laboratory to take measurements, analyse data, and produce reports. They can be used in mathematics instruction to graph equations, do calculations, and display statistics. Computers can also be an excellent information source. Word processing is another important use of computing as a support tool. A vital part of school education involves working with words. Preliminary studies indicate that use of word processing changes the way students go about composing and revising written work. Many educators expect students who use word processing to develop writing skills more quickly.

Computer Literacy

Computer literacy is a banner under which many of these arguments take place. Various definitions of computer literacy include the ability to program in a language, in most cases Basic; to use computers as tools; and to make sound judgements about the appropriate use of computers for a society as a whole.

At the elementary school level, the students' best introduction to computers is simply to use them and to see teachers using them. The typical student in an elementary school that has computers spends only 15 to 30 minutes per week with the machine, so the primary effect becomes exposure rather than delivery of content.

Keeping computer literacy in view, Government of India is making every effort to introduce computers in every secondary school by the end of the Seventh Plan under the name of a CLASS Project. A computer in every school is very good. But how about the colleges? The UGC does not expect itself to be able to provide a computer to every college in the country even by the end of the Seventh Plan and that would take us to 1990.

Framework for Manpower Development

Considering the issues discussed above, the following components may be adopted for manpower generations:

(a) *Generation of fully qualified scientists, engineers and software professionals*

These persons would have to go through a formal education programme in computer science and engineering and the exit level may vary from bachelor's to doctoral. They would meet the needs for senior software/hardware engineers, systems analysts, systems programmers or scientists in research establishments.

(b) *Training of degree-holders from other streams*

A large number of students who graduate in engineering, mathematics, science, commerce, etc. with reasonable exposure to mathematics can be trained in a formal system as programmers and systems analysts. With systematic training in the formal aspects of programming techniques and software engineering, these students could be moulded into capable application area specialists in their respective fields.

(c) *An integrated programme to meet the small user requirements*

An integrated B.Sc. consisting of courses in Mathematics, Physics and Computer Science at the first degree level would meet the requirements of small installations which are likely to grow in large numbers in the coming years. These graduates would also meet the requirements of computer teachers in schools/IITs.

(d) *Training of maintenance technicians and junior level programmers*

With the widespread use of small and large computers in all kinds of business and industrial applications, there will be an acute shortage of maintenance technicians. This could be met by introducing suitable hardware training courses at polytechnic level. To meet the immediate requirement, this may be started as a part-time course of one year duration and subsequently converted into a regular diploma. This part-time course may be started with participants who already possess a diploma from a polytechnic.

(e) *Vocational training*

A large portion of the manpower requirement relates to computer operators and data preparation personnel. These personnel can be trained at vocational training institutions like IITs.

In-service Training of Public and Government Sector Employees

The government and public sector organisations/departments will account for a major portion of the end-user groups. Since these organisations employ a large number of qualified persons, the training of selected employees of these groups in computer usage assumes great importance. A well organised plan of action for training employees of both government departments and public sector undertakings is essential. The duration of training may vary from one week to one year, depending upon the nature of the training and level of the participants. In-service diplomas could also help in meeting the immediate requirement.

Computer Literacy Programmes

Public awareness about the importance and use of computers is scanty at present. To popularise the use of computers, it is essential that the public in general, and the employees of government and public undertakings in particular, should be be able to appreciate information as an economic commodity. The government should therefore take necessary steps to spread computer literacy among the general public.

Crash Programmes for Teachers Training

It was felt by the Group that immediate steps must be taken to start training teachers with the requisite skills and abilities so as to facilitate the large-scale introduction of computer courses throughout the state. The existing teacher training facilities were assessed by the Group as being inadequate for the purpose. It is, therefore, recommended that short-term vacation courses be organised for training teachers from different levels of academic institutions.

Proposals for Faculty Generation

Teacher performance is the most crucial input in the field of education and training. Whatever be the course design and resources provided, in the ultimate analysis, these have to be interpreted and implemented by teachers.

Since the linkage of technical education with the growing manpower requirements of the computer industry has remained weak, adequate training facilities have not been introduced in the educational institutions. This has resulted not only in an acute shortage of manpower for industry, but also in a paucity of trained teachers for educational institutions. Even those who undergo formal training do not look upon the teaching profession as a desirable career option in terms of remuneration as well as status.

As a consequence, the centres which are currently offering computer courses have faculty drawn from various departments having little or inadequate computer training. This presents a sorry picture of the present status in a field which is technologically intensive and where the changes are very rapid.

[illegible]

[illegible]

[illegible]

[illegible] the [illegible] computer [illegible] ... [illegible] for the purpose [illegible]

Research [illegible]

[illegible] in the field of educa- tion and training. [illegible] design and [illegible] provided on the [illegible] to be [illegible] and implemented [illegible].

Since the linkage of [illegible] education with the growing man- power requirements of the computer industry has remained weak, [illegible]

[illegible] the various departments having [illegible] computer training. This presents a sorry picture [illegible] in a field which is technologically intensive and where changes are very rapid.

20

RECOMMENDATIONS FOR AREAS OF FUTURE RESEARCH

After all the presentations were over, the seminar participants discussed in detail the major areas of research. Ecah sub-group made separate recommendations which was integrated and presented as a final recommendation by the entire group. The same are reproduced here.

I. What types of computer applications have been developed for use in various areas of universities? (Preparation of an inventory).

II. What types of computer education will be needed in future, in India and Canada, in order to:

- meet future demands for computer users.
- advance our technology and societies.
- demystify computers.

III. Computer Awareness:

- How can it be maintained and increased most effectively?
- To what degree should it be developed?
- In what areas should people be trained?

IV. What are the priorities for the use of computers within universities? (including priorities for equipment, time frameworks, accessibility, etc.) and with specific reference to:

- teaching
- research
- administration
- interactive communications and networking

What have been the priorities and how might they change in the future?

V. What are the positive and negative impacts of the computer on:

A: teaching and learning
(How can the computer best be used for teaching and teacher training?);
B: research;
C: university administration; and
D: interactive communications and networking in a university setting?

VI. What will be the impact of *not* using computers on universities of the future?

VII. What is, and will be, the impact of computer education and usage in universities, on society as a whole?

- How can computers help make the educational opportunities available to as many people as possible? And to different language groups?
- How can computer education be developed so as not to further stratify our societies between the educated and uneducated?
- What kind of assessment models need to be developed for the study of the impact of computer technology in universities?

VIII. What are the decision-making processes that are needed for the further development of computer systems in Canadian and Indian universities?

IX. What impact will budgetary considerations have on the development of university computer systems, and how can they best be balanced with the priorities?

X. What are the problems and potentials associated with domestic computer and software production in Canada and India?

APPENDIX I

SEMINAR ON COMPUTERS IN INDIAN UNIVERSITIES

(11-14 February, 1987)

DEPARTMENT OF EDUCATION
South Gujarat University, SURAT-395007

PROGRAMME

February 11, 1987 (Wednesday)

10.00 am to 11.00 am	Registration		
11.00 am to 12.30 pm	Inauguration		
12.30 pm to 2.30 pm	Lunch hosted by Professor Mukund Trivedi, Vice Chancellor, South Gujarat University, Surat		

SESSION I

	Chairperson	:	Llyod Barber
	Rapporteur	:	Binod C. Agrawal
2.30 pm to 3.45 pm	Presenter	:	P.G. Reddy "Computer Man Power Development: Indian Scene"
3.45 pm to 4.15 pm	Tea/Coffee Break		
4.15 pm to 5.30 pm	Presenter	:	L.R. Symes "Computer technology in Higher Education in Canada"

February 12, 1987 (Thursday)

SESSION II

	Chairperson	:	Vimal Shah
	Rapporteur	:	Gail Moore
8.30 am to 9.45 am	Presenters	:	W. Stahl "Computer Literacy and Beyond"
		:	B. Majumdar

"Computer Literacy in Schools"

9.45 am to 10.15 am	Tea/Coffee Break		

SESSION III

	Chairperson	:	Ronald Miller
	Rapporteur	:	Man Mohan Singh
10.15 am to 12.45 pm	Presenters	:	C.S.R. Murty "Need to Look on the other Side of Computerisation"
		:	B. Maguire "Where is Technology Headed?"
		:	Ratna Ghosh "Educating Through Computers: Methodology and Impact"
		:	Vinayshil Gautam "Impact of Computerization of Work Design: Perspective on an Indian Experience"
12.45 pm to 2.30 pm	Lunch		

SESSION IV

	Chairperson	:	Gunvant Shah
	Rapporteur	:	B. MacDonald
2.30 pm to 3.45 pm	Presenters	:	W. Stahl "Technology and Values : An Assessment"
		:	Binod C. Agrawal "Social Impact of Computer Technology"
3.45 pm to 4.15 pm	Tea/Coffee Break		

SESSION V

	Chairperson	:	S.R. Thakore
	Rapporteur	:	Ashis Gupta
4.15 pm to 5.30 pm	Presenters	:	Lloyd Barber "The University of Regional Experience: A Laboratory of Success and Failure"
		:	L.R. Symes "Management Implications : Computers in Administration"

February 13, 1987 (Friday)

SESSION VI

	Chairperson	:	W. Stahl
	Rapporteur	:	Ameeta Jadav
8.30 am to 9.45 am	Presenters	:	B. MacDonald "Computers and Humanities"

		:	S.S. Raghavan "Microcomputers as a Laboratory Equipment"
9.45 am to 10.15 am	Tea/Coffee Break		

SESSION VII

	Chairperson	:	Ashis Gupta
	Rapporteur	:	Ratna Ghosh
10.15 am to 12.45 pm	Presenters	:	B. Maguire "Dealing with Distance: Educational Challenge"
		:	P.R. Reddy "Organizational Setup of Computer Education in Universities"
		:	Gail Moore "The Information Age and the Mandate for Research"
		:	R.R. Bryant "Public Policy and High Technology, with special reference to Higher Education"
12.45 pm to 2.30 pm	Lunch		

SESSION VIII

	Chairperson	:	Ratna Ghosh
	Rapporteur	:	B. Majumdar
2.30 pm to 5.00 pm	Presenter	:	Rekha Jain and G. Raghurama "Strategy for Promoting Computer Literacy"
3.30 pm to 4.00 pm	Tea/Coffee Break		

Workshop Issues

Workshop Discussion and Outlining Seminar Reporting

7.00 pm Dinner Hosted by Dr. Gunvant Shah and his colleagues

February 14, 1987 (Saturday)

SESSION IX

	Chairpersons	:	Ronald Miller Gunvant Shah
8.30 am to 10.30 am	Group Reports		
10.30 am to 11.30 am	Concluding Remarks – Canada – India		

APPENDIX II

MICROCOMPUTER AS A LABORATORY EQUIPMENT (Discharge of a Capacitor through a Resistance)

S.S. RAGHAVAN

Introduction

In India, microcomputers (also called micros) are finding a rightful place in colleges and higher secondary schools. Computer Assisted Instruction (CAI) and Computer Based Learning (CBL) are extensively used in developed countries for better learning by the students. In our country too, these methods are finding their place, though slowly, in teaching methodology. Apart from these uses, micros can also be used in a laboratory to control equipments and to measure physical quantities accurately and rapidly.

Many physical quantities such as pressure, voltage, etc. are measured using an analogue device to record their variations in experiments. All these quantities can vary continuously over some range and are usually measured by an instrument. The accuracy of such measured quantities depends on (i) the accuracy of the calibration of the instrument, and (ii) the interpretation of the observer. Measurement using digital techniques can be very accurate and if both analogue and digital techniques are combined, then we should have the method of recording a continuously variable quantity to a high degree of accuracy. This technique is called the Analogue to Digital Conversion and is used in most microcomputers. Since accurate measurements of quantities such as voltage, time, etc. are possible using a micro, many science experiments can be interfaced with it.

At Regional Engineering College, Mysore, I have tried out a few experiments successfully by interfacing with a micro. These experiments can definitely help the students to acquire a good understanding of concepts which are developed in the classrooms. In this paper, I describe one of these experiments, namely, the charge decay of a capacitor through a resistor.

Experimental Set-up

A BBC (Model B)/SCL Unicorn[1] microcomputer system is used for this experiment. This micro has an Analogue to Digital (A/D) port (Fig. 1a) through which we can measure small changes in voltages in a fraction of a second (as small as a centi-second).

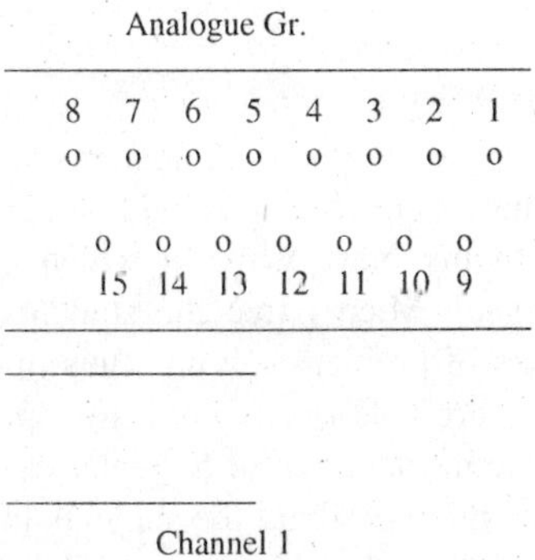

FIG. 1(a)

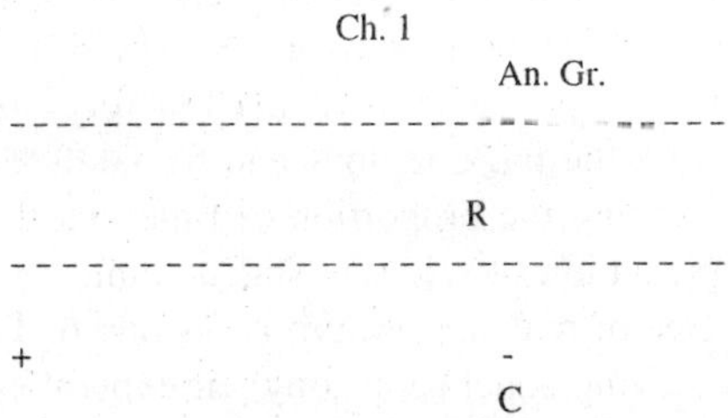

FIG. 1(b)

A/D Port Connections

A computer program (software) written in BASIC[2] is loaded into the computer via a Disc/Cassette drive and is run. The monitor screen (called Visual Display Unit) then displays a short description about the experiment and requests the user to enter the values of the capacitance and the resistance. The capacitor is now charged using a dry cell (1.5V). (Note that for this computer, the maximum allowed voltage input is 1.8V.) The battery is then disconnected and the charge in the capacitor is allowed to discharge through the resistor and the output is fed to the A/D port (Fig. 1b) of the micro.

The computer records the values of voltage as a function of time and the points are plotted on a voltage-time graph, which is displayed on the monitor screen. At the end of one minute, the computer plots the logrithmic value of voltage against time on the top corner of the monitor screen. This is a straight line graph from whose slope the user can evaluate the time constant of the given C-R combination. The experiment can be repeated a number of times and a mean value for the time constant can be found out. In this experiment, we find that the agreement between the theoretical and experimental values of the time constant is excellent.

Unlike with other methods, in this (computer based) experiment, we can also determine small time constants of the C-R combinations. Further, with this experimental set-up, it is possible to determine the accurate value of either C or R, if one of them is a known quantity.

Conclusion

We have described a simple experiment in which micro-computers can be used so that students can check the results obtained with other (usual) laboratory methods. There are many other ways in which a micro can be used in a laboratory course[3]. Micros free the students from the more tedious and trivial aspects of problem solving, thus increasing the proportion of time that they are able to devote to the appreciation of science. This amounts to the introduction of a greater degree of realism into problems posed. The micro will aid the students in drawing conclusions on their experiment before the class is over. There will be enough time for the students to discuss their result with the teacher. Such activities would have been impossible in a normal laboratory class. Thus micros act as a good companion to a learner in the laboratory.

NOTES

1. SCL Unicorn is a micro-computer system manufactured by Semi-Conductor Complex Limited, Chandigarh (India).
2. The software was developed by the author.
3. S.S. Raghavan, (1986), *Microcomputers in Science and Language Teaching.*

INDEX